# WORLD'S TOUGHEST *Rodeo*

# WORLD'S TOUGHEST Rodeo

## HOW ONE COWBOY BLAZED A TRAIL FOR WESTERN SPORTS

### TED HARBIN with STEVE GANDER

W. Brand Publishing
NASHVILLE, TENNESSEE

W. Brand Publishing is committed to publishing works of quality and integrity. In that spirit, we are proud to offer this book to our readers; however, the story, the experiences, and the words are the author's alone and portrayed to the best of their recollection. In some cases, names have been changed to protect the privacy of the people involved.

Copyright ©2025 Ted Harbin and Steve Gander

All rights reserved. No part of this publication may be reproduced, distributed, or transmitted in any form or by any means, including photocopying, recording, or other electronic or mechanical methods, without the prior written permission of the publisher, except in the case of brief quotations embodied in critical reviews and certain other noncommercial uses permitted by copyright law. For permission requests, write to the publisher, addressed "Attention Permission Request" at the email below.

j.brand@wbrandpub.com
W. Brand Publishing
www.wbrandpub.com

Cover design by JuLee Brand / designchik

*World's Toughest Rodeo* / Ted Harbin with Steve Gander —1st ed.

Available in Hardcover, Paperback, Kindle, and eBook formats.
Hardcover ISBN: 979-8-89503-061-5
Paperback ISBN: 979-8-89503-026-4
eBook ISBN: 979-8-89503-027-1
Library of Congress Control Number: 2025919170

# CONTENTS

Foreword: Telling the Story of Rodeo's Innovator ......... vii
Chapter 1: A Presidential Parade of Rodeo Stars ............ 1
Chapter 2: Work Ethic Forged by Family ........................ 9
Chapter 3: Rodeo Sparks Gander's Passion .................. 15
Chapter 4: Sales Jobs Guided a Future ......................... 23
Chapter 5: Building a Rodeo Business ........................... 29
Chapter 6: Rodeo on Ice .................................................. 37
Chapter 7: Rodeo Returns to the Big Apple .................. 43
Chapter 8: Prelude: Building a Team and a Business ....... 51
Chapter 9: Finding the Right People .............................. 59
Chapter 10: The Gander Approach ................................. 81
Chapter 11: Marketing a Different Product .................. 117
Chapter 12: Gander the Consultant .............................. 127
Chapter 13: The Dollor Bet ........................................... 139
Chapter 14: Side Shows ................................................ 145
Chapter 15: Other Productions .................................... 151
Chapter 16: World's Toughest Beyond Gander ............ 159
Chapter 17: The Gander Twilight ................................. 169

**About the Authors**

Ted Harbin .................................................................... 177
Steve Gander ................................................................ 178

## FOREWORD

# TELLING THE STORY OF RODEO'S INNOVATOR

The dancing lines and shadows twirled out of the burning end of Steve Gander's cigar as he took a sip from his red plastic cup, the perfect holder for the setting. He was lounging in a foldable lawn chair just outside his makeshift home—a horse trailer outfitted with living quarters and a tiny apartment-like section at the nose. The scent of Gander's tobacco intertwined with the embers in a barbecue pit a few feet away as cowboys and their families gathered at a post-rodeo meal in the small southeastern Texas town of Bellville. The air was filled with dust and the muskiness of the region's humidity, and there's always the lingering stench of bovine excrement and the ammonia-like dose of horse piss.

None of that bothered Steve Gander—he'd seen it all in rodeo. I sat there with Gander, Paul Riggs, and John Gwatney, silently sipping on a Coors Light while intently listening. I was the lone ranger in the midst of three cowboys who had long histories together. The tales—both tall and otherwise—had been shared many times, especially when they were together. They were mixed with long sips of good whiskey and bad, and the expressiveness and volume increased with more consumption.

John Gwatney's cackle gets to me. It's infectious, much like that of my wife. It stands on its own, the kind of noise that just brings a hint of a smile to anyone's face because we all know its genuine. When Gwatney is having fun, we're all having fun, dammit.

They have been braided together for decades. Whether they're sipping on good liquor or downing whisky sours—the Iowa version was mixing the liquor with Squirt soda—they always seem to have a good time together. The excerpts of their lives were how I learned more about Gander. It was fascinating. Between them, Gwatney and Gander are rodeo storytellers, a trait I dearly love. Theirs is verbal; mine is written. They spin yarns with decades of time in between; I conduct interviews and create prose about what I learned in those conversations. Nonetheless, there was always something in the back of my mind about presenting the details of an innovator and rodeo magician.

Anyone who has worked in the tightly wrapped rodeo industry for a few years has likely heard of Gander. In marketing the sport and producing events, he was doing groundbreaking things long before anyone else ever considered it. Whether it was introducing instant replays of the action like the big-time sports or having special openings and closings, Gander's goal was to keep an audience captivated. After selling both World's Toughest Rodeo and Dodge Rodeo in 2005, he leant his hand to help other entities succeed. He did it every time.

Alas, that wasn't the Steve I knew; no, he was the husband of Peggy, a professional photographer who focuses on Western sports. Through libations and those descriptive recollections, I became acutely aware of who he is, why his dream worked, and how others in the sport have been following in his footsteps.

Everything came to a head one hot August night in Lovington, a town of about 12,000 in southeastern New Mexico and the host of the annual Lea County Fair and Rodeo. It was Saturday night, and a group of 15 or so folks had gathered in the production building, a double-wide trailer that served as the rodeo secretary's office and substitute home for the gab session over five bottles of differing liquors and dozens of cans of beer.

Steve Gander had completed his task—taking down the lights his wife used to get the right shots through several nights of activities inside Jake McClure Arena during the nine-day exposition. He was ready for a drink and to return to the storytelling. We listened and laughed, and Gwatney cackled, as the tales got taller and the slurring became more prominent. It was then that Gander posed a simple question.

"Have you ever written a book?" he asked me.

With that, the wheels were in motion. Within two months, we were together again in a much more sublime setting in the southeastern Texas community of Hempstead, home of the Waller County Fair and Rodeo. Peggy was there shooting the rodeo, and Steve handled the driving, setup, and teardown. We spent more than six hours together over two days talking about Gander's life—from his meager beginnings on the family farm in northeastern Iowa, to starting a career in rodeo with hopes of being a bronc buster, to his eye for details. We discussed his first marriage, how a job selling dictionaries door to door forced him out of his shell, and how he opted to bet on himself and create a brand of entertainment that became World's Toughest Rodeo.

Just like many conversations we've had, there were a lot of laughs. Gander has that way about him, which makes him a phenomenal storyteller. Did I tell you he's already written a book? Oh, yeah; copyrighted in 2001, it's *Rodeo Event Marketing, The Business of Getting B.I.T.S. (Butts In The Seats)*.

It's a textbook, really, and it helps guide rodeo organizers on ways to help draw a greater attendance. There are some amazing tidbits, like how to avoid common pitfalls, ways to attract corporate sponsors, and what it takes to develop a strong advertising campaign.

My original idea was to be a ghostwriter for Gander, who had jotted his thoughts on a 40-page manuscript. As I read, I became more enthralled in his story. This needed a different touch. This needed more reporting, more detail. This needed more than his own voice. This needed research and time. I opted to author the book with Gander's help, utilizing journalism techniques I've used since my youth. The goal was to craft a bit of poetry for readers to enjoy. Journalism offers a different style than most novel writing, but I wanted to expand my voice, create more description, and bring together the sights, scents, and recollections of Gander's life through words.

Gander provided me with contacts, people with whom he'd worked over those years, from Kathi Myers, his first employee at World's Toughest Rodeo, to Mike Orman, the Dodge Rodeo rep who ran the operation before purchasing it from Gander in 2005. I had conversations with twenty to thirty people who spent parts of their lifetimes in his graces. I learned about Gander's brilliance and that he could be "damned abrasive and even very demanding, but he was never unreasonable," as David Morehead told me.

Throughout the process, I not only gained a better understanding of Steve Gander, but I also gained more respect for the man. His youth was an investment—he was the oldest of seven children born into a farming family in northeastern Iowa. Everyone was poor in that neck of the woods, especially those who toiled in the dirt and raised livestock in the 1950s and '60s. It was a hard life, but to the Gander clan, it was just life. They didn't know they were poor; they had what they needed, and love for God and one another was at the forefront of their home.

Through that, the family poured the foundation on which the eldest son built his platform. Much in the same way Catholics believe in the powers of Mary and God the Father, Gander held to his convictions. He prayed the Rosary and recited the Hail Mary, and he knew the phrase, "Bless us, O Lord, for these thy gifts which we are about to receive . . ." by heart by the time he was three years old. He also helped his dad, whether it was assisting a sow that was giving birth to a litter of piglets or driving the tractor to soften the soil. He dripped with sweat in July, when corn rows were filled with 8-foot-tall stalks and the sweltering heat mixed with the moistness in the air from the surrounding lakes, ponds, and rivers. Yes, there is such a thing as corn sweat, and he felt it. He also absorbed the stinging bitterness of winter when temperatures dipped well below freezing, but animals still needed human care. He used axes and spades to crack gaps in the ice so livestock could quench their thirst.

It was his life, his lifestyle, and with each slip in the pigpen muck and each nail hammered into a newly built shed, he stacked more blocks to his growing resume. It was in those fields and pens that Steve Gander became a man, someone who understood the importance of a good work ethic. It was the standard by which he charted the course of his life. Others may have been smarter, but nobody was going to out-work him, and he knew that. It's why he haphazardly built a desk in his basement and carried a kitchen chair down and up again daily in order to forge an empire.

None of those thoughts happen without Gander's revelations and the statements by those around him. Other insights came about through research, reading the lines scribbled decades ago about the history of rodeo or Gander's 1983 production of the Command Performance Rodeo for

President Ronald Reagan. Because of YouTube, I was able to watch the TV production from Landover, Maryland, and gather some amazing background, while also utilizing news reports about the rodeo to provide as much information as possible.

Every level of this project has been a work of interlacing passions: storytelling, rodeo, and personal friendships. The process yanked me out of my comfort zone while expanding the capabilities of my writing. It rewired my brain a bit, challenged me, and allowed me to grow in the work I do on a daily basis. I realized quickly that the focus necessary for this book was going to be more intense than I'd ever imagined, and I took the time required to purposefully put together the content to benefit Steve Gander and all he has done.

What I've learned the most is that Gander is a man with great dignity, and he's a friend to hundreds. He's genuine and loving—with grandchildren, step-grandchildren, and grandkids who aren't even related by blood. Over the course of writing this book, he has been my partner, driving me to be smarter and to write better. He's also supported me, whether I had to take a break because I was busy with my "day job" or hyping me up when it was time to officiate my daughter's wedding.

He's been more than a teammate, though; he's been a friend and a mentor. He's appreciated my talents and shared a passion for an unconventional sport that is based on the Old West. For me, it all goes back to storytelling—something at which Steve Gander excels. He's allowed me to do the same by writing it down in the pages that follow.

I'm honored to tell the tale of a true innovator in rodeo and Western sports. I'm honored to tell the story of Steve Gander, my friend.

CHAPTER 1

# A PRESIDENTIAL PARADE OF RODEO STARS

Deep in the bowels of the Capital Centre, the tires of a black limousine squealed as they were jockeyed into an awkward position by the chauffeur.

The driver's job: Back the oddly shaped vehicle down a skinny alley and onto the dirt-covered floor of the coliseum in Landover, Maryland. It was the first of several dry runs made by the operator, an agent with the Secret Service assigned to protect the President of the United States.

Rehearsals are vital for any show. Producers and actors need them. Technicians count on them. Inside the Capital Centre, virtually no one paid closer attention to pre-production more than Steve Gander . . . except for the agents in service to President Ronald Reagan.

Gander is a perfectionist who made a name for himself as a rodeo producer before he began coordinating the September 24, 1983, Command Performance Rodeo, which was inside the saddle-shaped auditorium in the Washington, D.C., suburb. The dry runs leading up to that spectacular event were necessitated by his attention to detail and the Secret Service's need to have the right plan in place should something dire occur. Agents were just two and a half years removed from being in the line of fire when John Hinkley Jr.

*1*

attempted to assassinate President Reagan. With thousands expected inside the coliseum, every precaution had to be in place.

"They had this brand-new limousine for the president, and they wanted to drive it into the arena and turn it around, but they didn't want to get it stuck," Gander said. "I suggested the driver back the limousine into the arena. They practiced backing it through the center gate and liked that they didn't have to turn around and were less likely to get stuck in case they had to pick up the President for security reasons."

Because of the limo's dimensions and weight, the arena layout, and the dirt flooring, reversing the vehicle into a predetermined spot had to be perfected for a quick exit. If the President were in harm's way, speed and precision would be a must.

As he watched the events unfold before him, Gander marveled at the synchronicity of it all. It was appealing to his nature. He is a man who brought together the Wild West and modern sports arenas, a marriage that some never expected but one that still exists decades later.

"I had booked the arena in Landover, Maryland, and we were doing the Pro Tour Finals in Casper, Wyoming," said Gander, a vibrant personality in his 70s, recalling how it all transpired. "I had the idea of doing the Command Performance Rodeo for President Reagan while we were in Landover."

Gander always had a way of making things happen. First, he conversed with Ken Stemler, the chief executive of the Professional Rodeo Cowboys Association (PRCA) at the time. Stemler reached out to a fellow rodeo cowboy, Malcolm Baldrige, who was President Reagan's Secretary of Commerce and a competing member of the PRCA.

With Baldrige on board, the details started coming together.

"A few more months went by, and I got word I was supposed to go to the White House and have a powwow with the Secret Service and the White House staff," Gander said. "I think it's the only time a professional sport did a command performance for a President."

As the day arrived, the White House staff set up a meeting between Gander and the President. Gander wasn't sure how the moment would come and go, but he was tickled to have the opportunity.

"I was in my production office and knew they were setting up for me to see President Reagan," he said. "I thought they would come to me and take me to his holding room, but then there was a knock on the door. I said 'Come in,' and this guy opens the door, and in walks Ronald Reagan.

"The thing I liked about him was that unlike a lot of politicians who look through you or around you, he looked you in the eye. He was genuine, and he knew I was from Iowa. He started talking about when he worked for WHO Radio in Des Moines. We got along great, and I gave him a World's Toughest Rodeo staff jacket, and he gave me a tie clip with the presidential seal and his signature on it. I still have his tie clip."

In the world of rodeo, it was a star-studded affair. Dignitaries filled the stands in Landover, and the arena floor was littered with world champions. Clem McSpadden, an Oklahoma statesman and rodeo-announcing legend, introduced the sport's greatest stars.

For most gathered in the audience, the stars were just cowboys. To those in the know, they were the elite of professional rodeo. The Command Performance Rodeo was the perfect opportunity to put their lives and talents on display for a new audience. President Reagan owned a ranch in California, and Baldrige shared the cowboys' passions as a team roper. Most everyone else was just there to be entertained. The exploits in and outside the arena were captured for a special television broadcast narrated by Hadley Barrett, another voice of the times and an eventual ProRodeo Hall of Fame inductee.

"What a thrill it is for us to see our Nation's leaders dressed in jeans, boots, and hats," Barrett said on the telecast. "It brings you a little closer to America because they look just like us."

That was no coincidence. It was a special day for all involved, including ambassadors from 46 countries. The event winners were awarded with presidential gold buckles, similar to the most cherished rodeo trophies. Most importantly, though, were the memories they made by performing in front of a crowd filled with policymakers and diplomats.

"There aren't too many activities in this land of ours with all the many things we do that are as purely American as we have seen here," President Reagan told everyone gathered after the rodeo ended. "We are very proud of all of you and grateful to you. A rodeo here on the East Coast I think establishes the fact that rodeos are now a national sport, not just a Western pastime. Madison Avenue, the advertising business, they found that out a long time ago; they found out Americans still love cowboys . . . and cowgirls."

He backed that up later during a special gathering for the contestants and other rodeo personnel on the White House lawn.

"The American cowboy remains a figure that is dear to the hearts of American people," the President said. "Men and women of the Old West may not be as slick as they were sometimes portrayed by Hollywood, but there is a certain integrity of character that shines through as we look back at them from the vantage point of history."

Making the event happen was a huge undertaking, but that was nothing new to Steve Gander. He relished in those roles, which is why many of the events he produced were so successful. The logistics of having a rodeo in Landover, Maryland, were intense. Where was the livestock going to be housed before and after the performance? What was it going to take to get the cowboys, cowgirls, and their animals situated? How many semi tractor-trailers was it going to take to bring everything into that coliseum?

That was just the rodeo side of it—the coordination of having an event for the President of the United States, his security detail, 11,000 dignitaries, and guests just added to the cluster of things that were going on for that special day. Gander met with both the Secret Service and the White House staff, and the PRCA administration to ensure every element of the day was covered long before the leader of the free world arrived at the Capital Centre.

"We had built a little viewing stand for the President, and every day the Secret Service would want us to lower it because they wanted to protect and cover the President," Gander said.

"Then the White House staff would come in and say, 'You've got to raise it by a foot.' Our crew would then raise the stand because the White House staff wanted the President to be seen.

"After like the second or third day of us raising and lowering the stand, my staff was just rolling their eyes every time somebody said to do something. I said, 'Don't worry about it; we'll just wait until the last possible minute and do what they tell us,' but we never ended up changing it again."

Other oddities came up that Gander and his crew had to handle. On the day of the Command Performance Rodeo, the White House staff called Gander to explain that the President's wife, Nancy, was not feeling well, and they weren't sure she'd be able to make the show.

"They asked if I could make sure there was something warm there for her if she were able to come," Gander said.

"I thought, 'A blanket? Here I am 1,500 miles from home, and I'm in a hotel. What in the hell am I going to give the First Lady?' But I said, 'No problem. We'll have something figured out.'

"I took off the bedspread from my hotel bed and brought it to the arena for her. She didn't come to the rodeo, but we had that bedspread there for her."

When it was time to clear the arena, Gander made sure to return the quilt to its rightful place. Borrowing hotel bedding wasn't the only memorable situation that day. Working with live animals can have its good and bad moments. During the rodeo, a bull got out of the arena and ran through the back pens in the Capital Centre and beyond—the animal was making its escape, running past Secret Service and White House staff vehicles parked on the ramp that bridged the inside of the building and the community of Landover.

"The bull ran by me . . . and there was this 6-foot-4 Secret Service guy that was about 250 pounds standing there by his van when the bull ran by him," Gander said. "This 250-pound man was trying to crawl up the antenna of the van when the bull goes up the alley with a pickup man right behind him. About 50 or 75 yards away was the presidential helicopter with two Marines standing by the steps of this helicopter with their guns.

"I was informed afterward that their job is to challenge anything that approaches the helicopter, but those Marines ran around the other side of the helicopter just as the pickup man roped the bull and brought it back to the arena."

Gander giggled at the recollection. There he was, producing possibly the most important rodeo in the history of the sport, and he witnessed two Marines figuring out how best to handle a charging bovine while standing watch over

Marine 1. The situation was handled as best as it could be, and the memories of that day will continue to occupy his mind.

There were more memories from one of the most celebrated days in ProRodeo history. The PRCA and event sponsors had a White House-hosted gathering. There was a barbecue, and the Command Performance Rodeo winners were issued their prizes by President Reagan on the South Lawn.

When he left, Gander talked his way into going through the White House and out the front gate to look for a taxi. On busy Pennsylvania Avenue, he and his first wife, Barb, realized the difficulty in finding a ride, so they began walking. Within just a couple of blocks, they managed to hitch a ride.

"This taxi is just barreling down the street before it slams on the breaks and slides over to the curb. A door swings open," Gander said. "A guy leans out and says, 'Hey, cowboy, you need a ride?

"It was a world champion bronc rider from South Dakota, Casey Tibbs. That probably wouldn't have happened if I wasn't wearing a cowboy hat. Tibbs said he saw a cowboy walking down the street and figured he was from the White House, so he just had the taxi pull over and get us."

In the Western lifestyle, cowboys take care of one another. It's common to see it on the big ranches in the Central Plains or in the timbers of the Rocky Mountains. It's rare in the Nation's capital. A helping-hand approach was the epitome of that weekend in many ways.

There were great costs in producing an event of that magnitude. Gander rented the Capital Centre and paid several thousand dollars in fees to make sure everything was presented in first-class fashion. His crew—the people that worked so hard behind the scenes at every Gander-produced event—managed the Command Performance Rodeo for free, and Gander lost a lot of money on the show.

"My company paid for the arena and all the staffing for ushering and all that, but it was about $40,000 to $50,000 out-of-pocket for those expenses," he said. "The crew donated their efforts for the performance. It was a day they will never forget.

"It was not about the money. It was about the experience."

In his lifetime, Steve Gander has had many amazing experiences. He wasn't raised to be a legendary rodeo promoter—he grew into one because of his experiences and his openness to try something new. His life story is about developing a brand, World's Toughest Rodeo, and building its success.

Not bad for a farm boy from northeastern Iowa.

CHAPTER 2

# WORK ETHIC FORGED BY FAMILY

Not far from the bluffs that overlook the Mississippi River in the Driftless Area of northeastern Iowa, rests the town of Postville. Near this community of 2,500 souls is where Earl Gander purchased his first farm in the early 1960s. His wife, Jean, and their children moved with him there, and they established a life of unending grace and service to others.

"I was raised near Waukon (Iowa) until I was 12, then we moved 15 miles away to the farm," said Steve Gander, the oldest of seven children. Had they lived in town, they would have boosted the population to nearly 1,600. The town has grown since then, but it still resembles much of what Small-Town America is like.

"Dad was a great father and educator. He was a man of conviction and faith, and he allowed his kids to make mistakes. He was not judgmental," Steve said.

Earl and Jean Gander gave their children what they had, which wasn't much. Life's lessons were the primary assets, and the value of hard work was a priority on the small operation that not only fed the growing family, but also people worldwide.

"We were poor, but we didn't know we were poor," Steve said. "Everybody in northeastern Iowa was poor at the time; Allamakee County was the poorest county in the state. My dad was an extremely good farmer, ahead of his time in management of livestock and that type of thing. After he died, we found all these awards that he received for seed corn, hogs, chickens . . . all these things that he was progressive in that he got from feed and seed companies.

"I love the farm, and I had always intended on staying on the farm. When I needed to have money, Dad gave each of us our own gilt, and we had a litter of pigs. We would keep so many hogs, and we had to pay for the feed and all that, and then we got the money when we sold the pigs. That's how I bought my own car, how I went to college."

The lessons that come with caring for animals are immense. Good stockmen make sure livestock and pets are fed before they themselves are. There's value in trudging through pig shit and helping momma cows give birth on the wettest and coldest of days.

"The work is enjoyable," he said. "You learn to enjoy that work is just part of your daily process, that work is part of life. Everybody can have pride in the job they do."

Steve Gander was born July 24, 1950. For many, life was simpler then. Not every home had a television, and entertainment options were fewer. There was more time with family, and that dynamic seemed to thrive. Faithful farmers didn't work Sundays, save for those daily chores that just had to be done. The other time was set aside for God and family, two beautiful entities for any man who grows food.

It's not glamorous, and it wasn't meant to be. On top of that, farmers in the 1950s and '60s didn't have modern conveniences that are available today. There was no air conditioning in tractors on those hot summer days or heaters when brisk, northern winds blew extreme cold and heavy snows. No, only the producers who could afford new equipment had them outfitted with cushioned seats, and there was no cab to protect anyone from the elements.

Steve Gander was seven years old the first time he drove the family tractor. That John Deere 50 was a precious commodity in Allamakee and Winneshiek counties sixty years ago. It not only helped till the soil and plant the seeds, it also provided a way to navigate the rugged terrain. Some of the pathways were basic trails between pastures or corn fields, so having a heavy-duty machine helped make for safer passages.

"We owned a cow that had a calf a little earlier than expected," he said. "I was on the tractor with Dad. We took the tractor out to the field to check on the cattle, and I was between my dad's legs. Dad had to pick up that calf to get the cow to follow him home, so he pointed the tractor toward home and put it in low gear. He shoved the clutch ahead and told me to keep it straight, and he jumped off. That was the first time I drove the tractor."

And it wasn't the last. Having the kids help with family farm operations was central to their way of life. It still is. All seven Gander kids knew what was expected of them, and in return, they received blessings from their folks. They also continued to receive lessons necessary to excel at the next stages of their lives. They just didn't realize it back then.

As the family's matriarch, Jean Gander had many roles. She was the at-home mom unless she was needed elsewhere. If they were baling hay, she drove the bailer. She ran errands to town for parts and other necessary items while everyone else handled the chores.

"With seven kids, she was busy cooking, too," Steve said. "I was the oldest, so I helped out with a little bit of everything. I got my orders from Mom *and* Dad. We all worked. I remember when I was 5 or 6 years old, we'd be washing eggs because it was our job to get the eggs from the chickens and wash them."

Being raised in a big Catholic family has its downfalls and its advantages, but they always found that the benefits stood out. Even when one of the kids went against their parents' wishes, Earl and Jean Gander remained judgment-free and willing to assist the youngsters through their misgivings.

"My parents taught me lots of lessons, but I'm not sure I learned them all," Steve said. "My dad had a great work ethic and never had a bad thing to say about anybody. If all hell broke loose, he didn't let it ruin his day. He just went on. I wish I was a little more like my dad in that regard. He was just so steady, so he got more done.

"If something ever bothered my dad, you couldn't tell that it bothered him. If he was disappointed in one of us kids, you'd never know. He was just so steady. My dad knew when he went to bed at night what he was going to do the next day. He probably had more done by 8 o'clock in the morning than most people do in a whole day."

Little eyes and minds catch more than most adults realize. Steve may have been the oldest, but his siblings also noticed the little things their parents did. Even his baby brother, who was sixteen years younger, transitioned from his life on the farm to develop a program that helped companies track shipments worldwide.

Their foundations had been laid along the same rows as the crops and pigpens on the family's farmstead. Just like her husband, Jean passed along her faith and dreams to the children. She prayed for her kids' growth and prosperity, just as she prayed for the crops and livestock that kept them clothed and put food on their table.

"Mom was the one who made sure we went to all the family gatherings," Steve said.

She made sure they kept up with their English lessons, knew their math facts, and could recite the Rosary and the Hail Mary.

"First communion was a big family deal," he said. "You had dinner with aunts and uncles and the cousins like you would on Thanksgiving. If there was any function at the church, we got together. We had priests at our house on Sunday all the time. My dad . . . he only went to school through fifth grade, and there were only five guys in the class; one of those was his year-younger brother, and the other three went on to be priests. They all stayed in northeastern Iowa.

"When my dad died, we had lunch after the funeral, and I went over and sat by my uncle Bill and monsignor Ed. I asked the monsignor to tell me some stories about my dad from when he was younger.

"Monsignor Ed said, 'A long time ago, your dad and I made a pact; I wouldn't tell on him, and he wouldn't tell on me.'"

The distinguished priest kept his word, and the message was clear: How Steve Gander was to remember his father was based on his own experiences with the man. He was okay with that, and he still marvels at his dad many years after his death. It's a deep love based on respect.

Steve Gander was raised to work and respect others. He cherishes those glowing moments that he shared in his formative years. His dad Earl was willing to step out of his own comfort zone to do things for his kids.

"My dad hated horses because he grew up working with them," Steve said, noting that his father's generation used animals instead of tractors to farm.

"We wanted horses so bad that when I was 13 or so, Dad had the neighbor find a horse for us, and that's what we got for Christmas. We knew nothing. We barely knew how to put a bridle on.

"On Saturdays, we'd do chores. If we weren't doing field work, we could come inside at 10 o'clock in the morning and watch *Roy Rogers*. I think that's why I learned to love horses. "

Steve Gander cherished those moments and the others he had with his folks after they'd retired from the farm. Earl loved to fish, though he hadn't done much of it when the kids were young—being a lone farmer and raising children kept him way too busy to venture off. With all that behind him, there was almost always a fishing pole in his hands.

"After Mom and Dad retired, I went fishing with them a lot," Steve said. "I took them out to the Lake of the Ozarks and rented a houseboat. Mom still talks about that as a great vacation."

The memories have lasted his lifetime . . . and hers. Much of who Steve Gander is lives in the beating heart of his mother, now in her 90s and still living in Iowa.

"Basically, she's quiet," he said. "She's a very hard worker but was unpretentious as a mother. She was not judgmental at all and was very steady. She was a good discipliner, but probably the best thing about her was her sense of humor. I think it's the Irish in her."

In his 70-plus years on this Earth, he has reflected on his upbringing. From a bountiful work ethic to an engrained curiosity, life on the farm and in the Gander family was the perfect form of education for Steve Gander. It is the guiding force he used to become one of the greatest promoters the rodeo scene has ever seen.

CHAPTER 3

# RODEO SPARKS GANDER'S PASSION

Cowboys of the American West were developed over time, but their foundation sprang from necessity.
   Old Westerns revealed the dusty and dry conditions most drovers endured as they cared for cattle, horses, and other livestock. That was surely the case in what became the American Southwest—the vastness of land that was previously part of the Mexican territory before throngs of eager pioneers settled beyond the Mississippi River.

The ruggedness of the landscape along the Southern Plains was altogether different than what cattle drives experienced in parts of Colorado and Utah, where paths were cut along mountain streams and rivers, across rocks, and over mountains. The vaqueros that tried to tame the Mexican territory were gifted horsemen who could do amazing things with a rope. They passed those skills on to their friends from the United States who became the first American cowboys.

Most of that lifestyle and livelihood resulted in a competitive demeanor among the men tasked with the work. Instead of playing card games, they competed to see who could rope or ride the best. The contests came straight from the range. Cowboys used their ropes to snare cattle in order to treat them for diseases, injuries, or to keep them close when they attempted to stray from the herd. Roping also aided in branding—a way to identify each cow by the insignia burned onto its hide.

As they attempted to add rideable horses to the mix, cowboys would try to tame their equine partners by "breaking" them. As was the case many years ago, humans would try to break the horses into submission by "riding the buck out of them." There were some ornery broncs—some even the greatest of hands had trouble staying on if they were bucking, snorting, and kicking. Those were the animals every cowboy talked about.

Like everything in the pioneer life, the daily work became the chessboard by which the cowboys played their games. Who was the best with the rope? Who could rope a steer and tie it down the fastest? Who could ride that bronc nobody wanted to try?

The roots of rodeo run deep. In today's society, it's a throwback to a way of life, but it's also a tip of the hat to the generations of people who founded this land. The sport's name is derived from the Spanish verb rodear, which means to encircle or round up.

The flair and bravado about those rough-and-ready cowboys was developed through various shows. *Buffalo Bill's Wild West Show*, which was developed by frontiersman "Buffalo" Bill Cody, provided a mixture of entertainment and education about Cody's life, work, and the cowboys, cowgirls, and others who aided in the development of the West. In shows that played nationwide in the late 1800s, hundreds of performers provided the context of the show while showing the skills necessary to handle the challenges that fell upon those that dared to make a life so far away from what many deemed "civilization."

The shows also used real cowboys and cowgirls who were recruited from ranches to brandish their skills before a crowd of people who paid to be entertained. The shows were so popular that Cody was asked to perform in England at Queen Victoria's Golden Jubilee celebration in 1887. Two years later, Cody and his cohorts were touring Europe.

Each layer of time transformed the labor of a working ranch into a piece of Americana entertainment and showmanship shown worldwide. Back home, the original work was becoming more intense. Community celebrations began including these pieces of the puzzle that eventually became the sport of rodeo, which has continued to gain participation and popularity.

By the mid-1960s, there were thousands of rodeos across North America. That's when Steve Gander was introduced to the pageantry and grace of rodeo. He and a high school buddy, Lowel Brandt, left their homes in northeastern Iowa to take in a little gathering just across the Minnesota border.

"I don't even remember the town, but I was hooked on rodeo," Gander said. "On the way home, I said I was going to be a rodeo cowboy."

The crossroads in life are more than intersections of chance. That little event in a small Minnesota community was the inspiration for one of the greatest minds to ever be involved in rodeo. Never mind that he hadn't finished high school or left the comfort of his parents' home—Steve Gander knew then and there what he wanted to do with his life. Determination filled his days of raising hogs and helping his parents and siblings on the family farm.

"It was the bronc riding and the bull riding, something I just wanted to try," he said. "When I was in college and 20 years old, I saw a poster for a rodeo near Waterloo, Iowa. There was a phone number for entries for the open rodeo, so I called the number and entered the rodeo in saddle bronc riding."

It made perfect sense to Gander, who was ill-equipped for the task. While attending college in Cedar Falls, Iowa, he went to the stables and told an employee there about his predicament: He'd already entered the rodeo but didn't have a saddle.

"He gave me a single-cinch, high-back saddle, and that's what I showed up with in Vinton, Iowa, for the rodeo," Gander said. "The stock contractor, Donnie Burkholder, took one look at that saddle and said, 'I can't let you ride in that saddle.' Donnie went to John Steenhook and asked him if I could ride on his saddle, and that's the saddle I used for my first horse."

That mount was 04 Missfit, which had been selected to buck at the International Finals Rodeo, the championship event for the International Rodeo Association, now known as the International Professional Rodeo Association (IPRA). Missfit was a mismatch for Gander, but it didn't matter.

"I think if I lasted three jumps, it's because it took me three jumps to fall off," he said, a wide grin spreading across his face. "I tell everybody, 'I landed on my head, and I've been involved in the sport ever since.'

"I popped right up, but when I went back to the bucking chutes, Donnie was looking down at me from atop the bucking chute. I peered up at him and said, 'Thank you.'"

Sure, it's how he was raised on a farm by parents who guided him and his six siblings, but it was also a sign of just how much he appreciated the opportunity. Not many would be as thankful for just having been manhandled by a farm animal, but Gander wasn't like most cowboys. That rodeo wreck was just what he needed. He started with a dream of being a cowboy, and that one episode in an arena near the banks of the Cedar River sparked a fire that never extinguished—he just didn't have the knowledge to become a great bronc rider.

Gander had an idea, though. A few days later, he reached back out to Burkholder for some insight and understanding of what it might take. Burkholder gave him that by bringing the young man to his place in Gilbertville, Iowa, a community of 750 just outside of Waterloo. It wasn't just training, though. It was work, and Gander was happy to do it. He wasn't afraid of hard work— that's how he was raised.

"I started working for Donnie—hauling hay, fixing fence, feeding, and doing everything else that was involved there," Gander said. "He would get a load of horses, usually from South Dakota, and Roger Mayo and I would ride those horses. Of course, we did it bareback, and we didn't have any pickup men, so we came up with a plan so the two of us could ride those horses."

The plan was simplistic yet genius. The rider would mount the horse in the chute, while the observer unlatched the chute gate. The rider would hold the gate closed while the other made his way behind that chute and flanked the horse. The rider would push the gate open, and the other pulled the flank to provide the leverage the horse needed to buck.

"The flank strap had a 20-foot rope behind it, so when you got bucked off or jumped down, we'd grab that rope and pull the flank once the horse stopped," Gander said. "Then we'd do it all over again."

The recollections brought back the vividness of those days. He could still feel the dampness in the humid air, smell the leather mixed with horse flesh that came with their attempts at greatness, albeit being in a lonesome arena in eastern Iowa. He never rode in front of thousands of fans at Cheyenne Frontier Days or the Calgary Stampede, but rodeo caught Gander's fancy, and his mind was set to do something special in the game he loved.

Aside from his work with Burkholder, Gander found other avenues to improve his skills in rodeo, whether as a cowboy or as the producer he eventually became. He began a post as laborer for Thyrl Latting, who had made a name for himself through productions across the Midwest. Latting was a rarity in rodeo. Not only was he part of Latting-Burkholder Rodeo Co., Latting Rodeo Productions, and Thyrl Latting Rodeo Spectacular, he was a Black man from Chicago. Over the course of rodeo history, a small percentage of Blacks have been involved. Only three Black men have won PRCA championships, bull rider Charlie Sampson and tie-down ropers Fred Whitfield and Shad Mayfield. Only two Black men were in the field of 120 contestants at the 2024 National Finals Rodeo (NFR), Mayfield and John Douch.

"Thyrl was a high school teacher in Chicago, but he was also a steer wrestler and a bull rider," Gander said. "His son, Mike, was a great college rodeo athlete, a tremendous bareback rider. He would ride bulls and steer wrestle and do just about everything.

"I pretty much helped gather livestock, sort livestock, and set up the arenas. Thyrl was a great mentor to me and one of the smartest men I ever met. He understood people better than anybody, maybe because of his background. Whatever it was, he did really well."

It was then that Steve Gander began to realize that there was much more to rodeo than just riding bronc or bulls. He began to pay attention to all the work behind the scenes and the manpower it took to make events like that happen. Gander started seeing the bright eyes and smiling faces in the crowd, and he bought into the idea that the sport of rodeo was not only a wonderful competition but also a way to entertain diverse groups of people.

"When I started going to rodeos and working them, I was more interested in the production of the rodeo and the spectators and everything else than I was becoming a world champion cowboy," Gander said. "I still have notes in my archives where I'd go to a rodeo and watch them park cars and try to figure out a better way to park cars because I didn't like how they were strung out in the streets. I would go to the concession stands at intermission and watch, and I determined you should not have more than two kinds of candy bars because a 12-year-old kid could not make up his mind if you had too many choices. That slows down the 15 minutes you had to make all your money."

That's simply a snippet into how Gander's mind worked and why he became the forefront producer in rodeo history. Long before he created the World's Toughest Rodeo brand, he was looking at ways to improve a product that had been around for several decades.

"There were things that I would look at as if I were a spectator at our rodeo," he said. "I used to tell our crew, 'Act like you're having a good time even if you're not. If you're walking down the arena going to the roping box, smile at those people in the front row, shake hands with them. If you act like you're having a good time, they're going to have a good time, too.'"

As simplistic as it seems, that behavior became contagious, and Gander thrilled hundreds of thousands of rodeo fans. It's why one-time visitors became repeat customers and why he is the guru of rodeo marketing to this day.

CHAPTER 4

# SALES JOBS GUIDED A FUTURE

By the time Steve Gander set off to college, life on the farm and working with family had helped create a bubble in which the young man had enclosed himself. While respectful, he was still shy and uncomfortable around others. Conversations were a struggle, and there was no eye contact with others, especially folks he didn't know well. Good conversations were reserved only for those closest to him. He spent more time looking at the toes of his boots than those with whom he was engaged.

In spite of that, he developed a friendship with another young man, Gary Grossman, who was a door-to-door salesman. Long before there were major retail chains popping up in small communities and well ahead of Amazon, home-to-home sales were how many companies marketed their products. Millions of encyclopedias and vacuum cleaners and kitchen knives were sold by people who knocked on doors for a living.

Grossman sold dictionaries and was fairly good at it. He thought his buddy could do it, too, so Gander took a job with Southwestern Publishing selling dictionaries door to door. One summer in the late 1960s, he was walking house to house in Tyler, Texas. He was learning how to approach people—completely unfamiliar ones. He was learning how to be persuasive and how to sell. He was learning things about himself that he'd use for the rest of his life.

And he was mildly successful. He earned the award for the most average number of demonstrations per week and was recognized for sales. He also earned some other honors because of the work he was doing, but it was less about his comfort level in communicating with others and more about the goals he had set for himself.

Gander didn't allow his shyness to become an obstacle to his tasks. His insecurity was a mere challenge to overcome, just as he had done on the farm as a youngster. Nobody wanted to endure the foulness that comes with raising animals and crops, but there was a job to do. If a sow needed help birthing her farrow, he had to wade through the muck and give her a hand. If the pickup was stuck in the mud, someone had to crawl through it to hook the chains so the tractor could pull it out.

Throughout that summer in east Texas, he wasn't growing corn or weaning calves. He was building his mind and his personality, able to convince housewives and homeowners why the Southwestern Publishing dictionary was just what they needed. He walked hundreds of miles over those months, but he didn't return home at night until he'd reached the goal he'd set for the day.

"One time in Tyler, it was raining cats and dogs," he said. "I was at a gas station, and I still had one more demonstration to make before I could go home. It was like 8 o'clock at night, and a policeman comes into the station. He'd seen me several times that summer walking around, going door to door, so he started a conversation with me.

"'Do you want a ride home?' he asked. I said, 'Well, I can't go home yet; I've got to do one more demonstration.'

"He replied, 'You can give me a demonstration while I drive you home, but I'm not going to buy.'

"A few days later, I happened to knock on his door, and his wife bought the books from me."

The grin on Gander's face was wide as he reflected on that rainy day in east Texas. What proved to be the fork in the road was what the man needed to take. The lessons he gained while developing callouses on his knuckles became another cornerstone in the life he was building.

He returned to a more familiar life back in Iowa, but he continued to utilize the skills he gained while selling door-to-door.

"At the time, I was working at the sale barn part-time and this old guy—I thought he was a scalper—would show up at the end of the day with some cattle to sell the next day," Gander said. "He could hardly get from his truck to the back of his trailer. He had his own pen for cattle that he always brought for the sale, so I'd take the cattle back and make sure they had water. If someone didn't use all the hay they had, I'd throw some hay over the fence for the calves.

"After a few weeks, the old guy must've noticed I was doing something, so he offered to buy me lunch. I had lunch with him a few times, and I started asking him some questions. I remember one time I said, 'I don't know how you make money scalping cattle.'"

Gander's assumption was that the old-timer was buying cattle from another entity, either from another sale barn or from a livestock producer, and hoping to resale the animals for a quick profit. He couldn't have been more wrong. Though he dressed "raggedy" and drove an old truck pulling an old trailer, the old man was one of the sale barn's primary owners. Gander had made his mark, and within days of that lunch, the older gentleman told the sale barn manager to hire Gander full time.

"He told me, 'As long as you keep doing something, you'll succeed at it, but if you're losing money and you quit, then that's money you'll never get back. You can only get it back the way you lost it, so don't give up.'"

It could be an epitaph for fortitude and resilience. The exchanges he had, whether doing a little extra for a client or having lunch with an older gentleman he didn't rightly know, added another layer to his life. The old-timer's words were ones that could be carved into stone and made available to all who needed or desired to read them.

"One of the morals of his stories is to always be kind," Gander said.

Fate was turning his life around. His work ethic and personality were opening eyes of influential people. A former Southwestern Publishing sales manager had changed jobs and was working for Security Hybrids Seed Co. The manager learned about Gander's prowess, and knowing Gander was from Iowa, he reached out to fill a need for a regional salesman.

"I wasn't there very long before they made me regional manager," Gander said. "They created three regions, and two other guys were there before me. They each had a region, then made a third and put me in it. The first year, my regional sales outgrossed each of the other two regions. After that, they moved one guy into my region and moved me into his region. That year, I was again number one in sales. I never let anyone outwork me.

"It wasn't the number one region at the time because it was a bigger area, and I was the only guy that was single and was willing to travel as much. I made that region the number one."

He and his first wife, Barb, got married shortly after the changes were made. Sales were still skyrocketing, but despite the success, Gander's rewards weren't as great. He learned through office-talk that the other two regional managers made more money than him. Gander went to the general manager and learned that it was true.

"The GM told me that the president of Security Hybrids thought that because the other two had children, they should get more," Gander said. "I believed I worked harder than the other two and told the GM I was going to resign. I said that I could leave that day, put in a two-week notice, or, if they wanted, I would stay until the kickoff meeting in July with the condition that the company would pay for my parents to go on the company trip to Ireland."

The general manager wanted to visit with the company's president before responding. That was okay with Gander, who received calls that evening from the president and vice president asking him to reconsider.

Gander's parents got to go to Ireland. Meanwhile, Security Hybrid executives decided to sweeten the deal for their top salesman and offered him a position as vice president in charge of international sales. Gander and Barb ventured to California, where the company gave them a Mercedes-Benz to drive around while pondering their futures. The operation was impressive, especially to someone who knew the products as well as Gander. Security Hybrid bred seeds and had success with alfalfa, cotton, and had begun dabbling in corn.

Gander was offered $50,000 and a car—a huge deal in the 1970s. At value, it would be worth $300,000 or more today. It was the opportunity of a lifetime . . . until it wasn't. There was more to consider, so on the way back to Iowa, Gander did.

"I told my wife, 'If I'm worth this much money to them, how much money would we be worth to ourselves if we do our own thing?' I told her I'd like to be a rodeo producer. They offered me $50,000 and a car, so it was a big deal. We landed in Denver, and I called the banker to come meet me at the airport in Cedar Rapids and bring me home from there. On the way, I told him what I wanted to do.

"He said, 'I don't understand being a rodeo producer, but your boss speaks very highly of you.' They lent me $15,000 to start my company based on my reputation."

In a small country town, it's a farmers' bank, an indication of its biggest clientele where a young man is judged by his dad. Loans are based on the business of farming, a trade that tends to be handed down through the generations. If the father was a good farmer, then the young man had a chance of getting a loan. If he wasn't a good farmer or was the town drunk, the young man didn't stand a chance at a loan. Reputation is everything in a small community.

In Gander's case, he wasn't from that community. He grew up 100 miles away, and so was his family's stature. The bank's dealings with Gander's company, though, made the difference. It came in handy when he started with Security Hybrid because he didn't have the clothes necessary to be in sales. He told the boss, who co-signed Gander's first loan.

"I went to the bank and got a $300 loan so I could buy clothes for my job," Gander said, adding that because he was always the top salesman for the company, his boss put in a good word to the banker. "I'm positive that my work ethic and my efforts are what got me that loan.

"What you do today helps you tomorrow. I'm a firm believer in that."

CHAPTER 5

# BUILDING A RODEO BUSINESS

A $15,000 loan in today's world wouldn't cover a year's worth of mortgages, but in the late 1970s, it provided a meager start for Steve Gander's ProRodeo Enterprises. He didn't need a lot—all he needed was his idea. He'd already produced one rodeo in Des Moines, Iowa, a few years prior, but he left corporate America to test his business plan with nothing but his will to make it happen.

Barb, Gander's former wife, felt a bit uneasy. A week after he'd set a new course for them, the Ganders learned they were expecting a baby, a loving contribution to the family but another mouth to feed and a motivating factor in his drive to overcome any challenge. He charged through every barrier like it was smoke, even if flames licked at his heels.

"It was scary, but it scared Barb more than it did me," he said. "I was going to do the work I needed to do. My desk was a sheet of plywood on top of cinder blocks down in the basement. Every day, I'd take one of the kitchen chairs to the basement as my office chair, and at the end of the day, I'd take it back up."

He'd scratch and claw his way to the top. He took the loan money and invested in producing a rodeo in Ames, Iowa, home of Iowa State University, a land-grant college with strong academics in agriculture and veterinary medicine. It was an ideal location for the first event of his upstart production company.

"It took a lot of work and a lot of luck to pull that off," Gander said. "We made a modest profit and paid the $15,000 loan off. I probably got some preferential rates from some of my rodeo friends for stock and everything else, but everybody got paid. My claim to fame is that when you work for me, you get paid. I don't think any of my employees ever had to worry about whether they'd get paid or not, even if we didn't have a successful event."

As strange as it may seem, employees of traveling road shows weren't always guaranteed a payday. If some promoters took a loss on an event, their workers did, too. Gander wasn't going to let that happen.

"One of the things I did early on was write all the checks, and I personally handed them to my employees before the final performance," he said. "They never had to come find their check after the rodeo. This was important to me. Paying my crew was something I looked forward to just to say thanks."

In his mind, it was vital. He needed the livestock providers, the timers, the crew behind the scenes, and other personnel to make the events happen and to provide the best entertainment value to the fans that paid to be there.

"I wanted them to be comfortable," he said. "I knew the reputation in the traveling-entertainment industry that a lot of people put on an event or rodeo, and if it wasn't successful, the people that worked there would be left standing either with a bad check that would bounce, or no check at all. That just wasn't going to be the case. It was a matter of pride for me."

Each step was one rung higher on a long ladder to success. Gander refused shortcuts. He wasn't just handling business;

he was doing business the right way. Employees earned their pay, and he wasn't going to short-change them. Most, if not all, were going to be hired again, and early on he wanted them to know he valued their involvement.

He wanted people to know their worth, so he established his own credo: "Saddle your own horse and cut your own trail. No sense in following someone else's trail. They probably don't know where they're going."

His "horse" was ProRodeo Enterprises–and later SMG Inc.–and the "trail" he cut was made by his own vision. His thoughts surged forward, crafting plans for something extraordinary. He began his journey on a familiar route in Iowa, but he expanded it because he knew the opportunities were there. Perceived barriers became blocks on which he built his resume.

"I don't consider it an obstacle, but the biggest thing was a lack of foresight and thinking by others," he said. "When I started my company, every rodeo was produced by a rodeo committee, a local thing. I didn't want to be beholden to someone else's budget for my success. I never had the patience for somebody else to make those decisions. My format was to underwrite and produce my own events. I felt like we could have better quality events, and we could go into bigger markets.

"I'd always wanted to be a farmer, but farmers are beholden to the Chicago Board of Trade. They work hard, they produce their crops, then someone else gets to determine what the price is. When I'm producing a rodeo, I get to determine the ticket prices. I'm controlling my own destiny, and I like that."

In governing his decisions, Gander kept score. He maintained intricate records and tallied his results to identify what worked and what didn't.

"I also have a better scorecard than most businesses, which is what they have or don't have at the end of the year," he said. "If I'm doing 20 rodeos, I get more scorecards, and I can add a few more scorecards. I can add a scorecard on how much sponsorship money I make. I can add a scorecard on how my merchandise sales do. It's easy to maintain momentum when you have all those scorecards throughout the year."

In his second year, Gander produced five events: Cedar Rapids, Iowa; Dubuque, Iowa; Austin, Minnesota; La Crosse, Wisconsin; and Minneapolis. His franchise was growing slowly, but it was developing at a pace that worked for Gander. Every stop became a stepping stone. Just like he did when he was working for those stock contactors in his younger days, Gander paid attention to every detail. He wanted parking attendants to be cordial because they were closer to the customer than any rodeo personnel. That first impression is important so the spectator is in the right frame of mind to have a good time when the rodeo starts. Parking attendants and ushers are closer to the customer than everyone else.

He was also seeking the right name for his rodeo tour. While producing an event in Des Moines, Iowa, he overheard a defeated cowboy who'd got bucked off a Thyrl Latting bronc saying something about the "World's Toughest." The name stuck, and a brand was formed.

"I wanted a name that could live beyond me," he said. "At the time, every stock contractor had their name in it: Latting-Burkholder, Sutton Rodeo, Korkow Rodeo, Jim Shoulders Rodeo. I wanted a name that would live after me, and I wanted a marketing name. In the 1980s, one of the greatest things I reflect on was the cowboys would say, 'I'm going to the PRCA rodeo,' or 'I'm going to the IRA rodeo,' or 'I'm going to the World's Toughest Rodeo.'"

In that era, the PRCA and the International Rodeo Association (IRA) were the premier sanctioning bodies in the sport. The PRCA had a little bit of a leg up on the IRA, but they were of similar stature. At times, World's Toughest Rodeo was aligned with one or the other, but the name stood on its own.

"With our marketing, we elevated our product's perspective," Gander said. "That alone is a measurement of success. In our mind's-eye, we naturally place things on the rungs of a ladder. The top rung in rodeo is the PRCA and the National Finals Rodeo. All other associations and individual rodeos are on lower rungs of the ladder. We succeeded in getting World's Toughest Rodeo on a higher run of that ladder."

The name remains one of the most recognized in rodeo. Today, there are several World's Toughest Rodeos spread from Des Moines to Columbia, South Carolina. The basis for each performance—whether it was in Cleveland 40 years ago or in Charlottesville, Virginia, today—comes from the little things Gander did when he founded the operation.

"I worked really, really hard on that first event in Minneapolis," he said of the 1980 World's Toughest Rodeo at the Metropolitan Sports Center, known as the Met Center. "I had a whole list of things for my business plan. We did not want to be known as a small-town producer. I worked really hard to get into big markets. I remember mimeographing letters to buildings. Every building got the same letter in consideration.

"Bob Reid was the manager of the Met Center. He responded to that mimeographed letter."

That set the wheels in motion, and the Gander train kept gaining speed. A few years later, Gander attended a convention of arena managers where Reid spoke. In his address, Reid told convention attendees that World's Toughest Rodeo was one of the most successful events at the Met Center.

"Bob said he made two mistakes," Gander recalled. "He said, 'Never before had I ever responded to a mimeographed letter, but for some reason, I responded to Steve Gander's. The biggest mistake was when Steve offered a partnership. I refused him and made a preferential rental agreement, and I would have made a lot more money if I'd have been partners with him.'"

That reference served as a launch pad for World's Toughest Rodeo. Gander and his team delivered on all the promises they made.

"We were honest and easy to work with, and the arenas never had to worry about anything getting done," Gander said. .

Word was spreading, but that only gained the attention of the people running arenas. He still needed to sell tickets, and that's where Gander's brilliance really took off. He took World's Toughest Rodeo on a wild ride of marketing, focusing on the best avenue to reach potential ticket-buyers in big cities. While many city events focused on advertising in the Des Moines Register, the Minneapolis Star Tribune, the Cleveland Plain Dealer, and handing out posters across the community, Gander took a different approach altogether.

"Posters and newspapers were the number one medium, but I determined that rodeo was visual and that television should be our number one marketing medium," he said. "I think most family shows and sports weren't doing television because they just didn't understand how to do the commercials. Most events used newspapers for 60 to 70 percent of an advertising budget, but I made it to where 60 percent of my budget was television.

"We took off like wildfire. We were actually copied by truck pulls and other different shows. Arenas would take our marketing program and share it with the other events, and it came to my attention that we were action. I always put the audience in my commercials. I want people to visualize themselves being at my arena."

Maybe it was his forte or his vision, but Gander did everything with a certain purpose and focus. He looked at his promotion, marketing, and production through the eyes of the audience.

"You've got to look at the arena from the perspective of the spectators," Gander said. "If we take care of the spectators, the spectators are going to take care of the cowboys and the sponsors and us. We put the rodeo on for the benefit of the spectators. A lot of people looked at it like they were putting on a rodeo for the benefit of drawing a world champion calf roper. That's OK, but that's not for the spectators' benefit.

"If I go to a rodeo and see a dusty seat, what I see is a lady sitting down in a brand-new pair of black slacks and getting those new slacks dusty. She will not come back to the rodeo. I want clean restrooms. I want the parking lot to be easy. I want the stadium seating to be clean, and the chutes and holding pens need to look like they can keep the Budweiser Clydesdales in them. Everything needs to look nice."

It's difficult to make so much of an arena look pristine, especially when dirt is added to the concrete floor by the truckload. His approach was like that of a chef who not only crafts spectacular dishes but also presents them in a way befitting a five-star restaurant. The plates are displayed with crispness, and the meals not only taste fantastic but are presented in a way that leaves guests marveling.

The thrilling action in the arena forms the entrée, the production adds the finishing flourish, and the whole experience leaves fans utterly satisfied.

CHAPTER 6

# RODEO ON ICE

The bitter cold that hits northeastern Iowa from late fall to early spring can be brutal. Frigid winds bring blasts of stinging cold, the kind of chill that ignites the skin upon its touch. Why do people live where the air hurts their faces?

It's especially harsh for those who aren't acclimated. Ask John Gwatney, who was raised between Arkansas and California and experienced his first arctic blast in the fall of 1998.

"The weather is not made for people who aren't interested in it," said Gwatney, who spent just seven months as operations manager for Steve Gander's World's Toughest Rodeo. "You have to want to do it."

Gwatney now lives in the southeastern Texas community of Marquez with his wife, Sandy. Back then, he was a rodeo cowboy who had a keen understanding of rodeo showmanship, and the opportunity to help produce events was more than intriguing. He was in charge of many aspects of the operation, from taking bids to making sure the dirt was right for each performance.

With Gwatney's assistance, Gander's crew put on sixteen rodeos in twelve weeks. It was hectic, wild, and overwhelming at times. There were four weekends in which they produced two events—which is no small task—and Gander not only appreciated Gwatney's talents but trusted him to handle the business as needed.

"I needed an arena director . . . we were getting bigger, a little more complicated," Gander said. "I wanted to take some burden off my shoulders. John became a manager for a lot of things, but he didn't stay very long; he didn't like the cold weather."

Gwatney left Williamsburg, Iowa, to continue his career as a professional rodeo cowboy. By that time in his life, he was wrestling steers. There's not much he hasn't done when it comes to rodeo, whether it was riding bulls or serving as an official, the sport's referee. These days, he's one of the most sought-after production supervisors, the person dozens of events count on not only to put on a competition but to also make it entertaining for a crowd.

He may have vacated his spot with World's Toughest Rodeo, but he still utilizes the skills he gained from that experience decades later. Now, though, he opts for warmer climates and doesn't have to deal with feet of snow or packed ice on the roadways nearly as often.

Gwatney wasn't the only one who shivered in the cold. Most everyone who came from a southern home felt that bitter chill, where windchills in northeastern Iowa have been known to dip to -55 degrees Fahrenheit. It's harsh, even for the most seasoned Midwesterners. It's more difficult for folks who prefer their winters mixed with sunny days, bright sunshine, and just a splash of cold moisture.

Extremely cold weather is reality in the Upper Midwest. Ponds and lakes freeze, dirt is solidified several feet deep, and vegetation becomes dormant for months at a time. There's a reason ice fishing is popular there and why ice hockey rules the roost in North Dakota, Iowa, Minnesota, Wisconsin, Illinois, Michigan, and Ohio. Northerners layer their clothing, lace up the skates, and find a convenient, frozen puddle to show off their skills.

Major coliseums learned how to create amazing rinks inside their massive walls. That offered another challenge for Gander as he was building a rodeo franchise. He knew he needed to put his shows in the Met Center in Minneapolis and Richfield Coliseum near Cleveland. The infrastructure was already in place to house thousands of fans and get them in and out of the complex in an orderly fashion.

"I did not want to be known as a small-market producer," Gander said. "To truly enhance potential for success, we needed to be in NBA and NHL arenas."

One of his first tasks was preparing an impersonal mimeographed letter that he sent to major-market sports arenas, which were spread across the country. One letter got a response: Bob Reid in Minneapolis.

"Thank goodness he didn't pre-judge me," Gander said with a laugh. "That one response led to a 30-year business relationship with the Gund Organization, which owned the Minneapolis North Stars of the NHL and the Cleveland Cavaliers of the NBA. They later owned the San Jose Sharks of the NHL.

"I headed to Minneapolis for a meeting; I wanted to secure first-quarter dates—January, February, or March—and ink a co-promotion with the arena. I didn't get either. The hockey schedule and other events already had the building booked, and a co-promotion was not feasible. They preferred to only rent the building, and I had no sports-facility production track record."

It was an ominous start for the start-up rodeo company, but Gander pushed onward. Despite his wishes, he took a May weekend under the assurance that if the Gund Organization liked the rodeo and business with Gander, it would consider having the rodeo during the NHL All-Star break the following January.

"In 1979, I learned that it took five to six days to make good hockey ice," he said. "How was I going to be a big-market rodeo producer when arenas couldn't take ice out because the ice-making systems were a slow process? Nowadays, there are more efficient systems in place to make the ice in a lot less time, but my dream to produce rodeos in major markets was getting crushed.

"That wasn't the only challenge. My first year in business, I had five events scheduled in the first quarter: Cedar Rapids, Iowa; Dubuque, Iowa; La Crosse, Wisconsin; Austin, Minnesota; and Bloomington, Minnesota. My erratic schedule events coincided with important days. My daughter was born the week of the La Crosse rodeo, Easter weekend was in Austin, and Mother's Day—along with the opening day of fishing season—was the weekend of Bloomington."

He survived despite his ignorance, but he gained valuable lessons: "Rule Number One in event marketing is to never compete with God or mothers. Stay away from holidays—Mother's Day, graduations, etc. And I needed to figure out a way to put dirt on ice and preserve the ice."

It wasn't Mission Impossible, but it wasn't a G-rated movie either. Gander began reaching out to people with a better understanding so he could figure out how to put dirt on ice. One major source was Frank Jirik, the operations manager of the Met Center and other arenas. That's when he found out that NBA floors and concert venues used homasote insulation on the frozen rinks. Gander continued to reach out to other arena contacts who were also hungry for answers. The economics for arenas weren't good in that era, so they were looking for solutions to book more dates. The operations managers were eager to help find the answers.

"We came up with a layering plan. Four-foot by eight-foot homasote insulation panels, then thick visqueen plastic, three-quarter-inch plywood, thick visqueen plastic over the plywood, then spread eight to ten inches of sandy, clay dirt on top of that," Gander said. "It worked pretty well. After a few tries, we learned not to use the top piece of plastic. We learned to modify the edge of the bucket on the excavator and turn the heat on the ice-making equipment while we were taking the dirt out. Once the ice softened on the top, it was easier to clean dirt specks out of the ice with the Zamboni machine."

One hurdle was cleared, but there was a long line of others in the path. Water isn't the only thing that freezes in a Midwestern winter. That proved to be another obstacle to overcome.

"We had to figure out how to get unfrozen dirt from January to March," he said. "Riverbank dirt became our first choice, and one way we went about it was to stockpile the dirt and cover it before the freezing winter hit. That was expensive, and it became difficult to find a place to store it.

"The way we usually did it was to dig down three to four feet below the frost line to get the unfrozen dirt. I don't remember the first time we did this, but arenas got word of it, and we started getting calls."

While trying to thaw dirt, Gander was also trying to take advantage of a hot subject in theater. The movie *Urban Cowboy* was released June 6, 1980, starring John Travolta and Debra Winger. It centered around the nightclub Gilley's, a honky-tonk near Houston that featured dancehall music and a mechanical bull-riding apparatus. It brought country living into city life, and it opened the door for many to buy jeans and wear pearl-snap shirts and look the part of a cowboy, even if it was just for a night out.

The movie also increased interest in the Western lifestyle and the sport of rodeo. While Donnie Gay was winning rodeo's gold, Travolta-wannabes were getting decked out in pointed-toe cowboy boots and heading out for the night. Country music was gaining popularity, and hordes of people were packing every fairground arena and rodeo complex to enjoy a bit of Americana.

"When *Urban Cowboy* came out, we were the hottest thing at indoor arenas," Gander said. "Businesses become successful when they recognize customers' needs and solve them. We thought outside the box and became a viable event to major arenas. We were an unknown commodity in rodeo, arena sports, and family entertainment.

"We took calculated chances, stayed loyal to our business plan, overcame obstacles, worked harder than anyone else, and became the largest privately owned rodeo and production company in the industry."

CHAPTER 7

# RODEO RETURNS TO THE BIG APPLE

The most populated city in the United States of America is about as far from the Old West as you can imagine.

Nearly nine million souls reside in New York City, with Manhattan having the highest population of the five boroughs. It's an island, really, enclosed by the Harlem, East, and Hudson rivers. Most of Manhattan is made up of concrete and steel. It's home to the Empire State Building, One World Trade Center, the Chrysler Building, Rockefeller Center, and masses of inhabitants who help make it one of the world's most influential cities commercially, financially, and culturally.

It is the epicenter of theater and business. Diversity reigns, and life is fast-paced. It's much different than the vastness of western Texas or eastern New Mexico, where ranches raise beef cattle in a desert climate. Life in New York City is paradoxical to the way families work in Killdeer, North Dakota, where harsh winters are just a way of life on the open ranges and grasslands.

There have been times when these two worlds collided, though, and it occurred for more than a century at a place just a half mile from Times Square.

Madison Square Garden was originally opened in 1879 and has been transformed multiple times. The existing building—between 31$^{st}$ and 33$^{rd}$ Streets and 7$^{th}$ and 8$^{th}$ Avenues on Manhattan's West Side—opened in 1968. The arena was recognized as a unique piece of engineering for its time. The venue has hosted the NBA Finals, the Stanley Cup Finals, and a variety of all-star games. It has been home to both Democratic and Republican national conventions and the 1971 "Fight of the Century," which featured heavyweight combatants Muhammad Ali and Joe Frazier. The NBA's Knicks and the NHL's Rangers still play there. Billy Joel performed inside the historic venue 150 times. Elvis, Madonna, Stevie, and Taylor have lifted the rafters with their brands of entertainment.

A century ago, the Old West found its way into the city via rodeo. Madison Square Garden was where world champions were crowned until the advent of the National Finals Rodeo, which was produced for the first time in 1959 at Dallas. Rodeo then vacated the massive arena, and it didn't really return in full glamor until Steve Gander brought it back in 1980.

"When I started my company, I wrote down goals I wanted to achieve," said Gander, who developed World's Toughest Rodeo in the late 1970s. "I mailed a handwritten copy of my objectives to Marty Martins, who was the editor of Rodeo News. He kept my notes and mailed it back to me years later. Today, they are stored in my archives.

"My objectives were, one, I wanted to become the biggest rodeo company in the IRA; two, I wanted to take rodeo back to Madison Square Garden; three, I wanted to make a contribution in the rodeo industry; and four, I wanted to have fun doing it."

With that written on a piece of paper Gander still has, he got the ball rolling. He reached out to Stetson, a hat-maker who was in New York City at the time and made the classic fedoras of the day but also sold a hefty number of cowboy hats. It was a sign of the times, thanks in part to the movie *Urban Cowboy*, a feeling of nostalgia from John Wayne movies, and a taste of the cowboy culture and Western lifestyle.

"Early on, I started working on getting rodeo back to Madison Square Garden by 1980," Gander said. "The first thing I did was go to Stetson Hats. It took me about a year, but I got Stetson Hats to become a sponsor, and they got us enthused about going back to Madison Square Garden. In 1980—with *Urban Cowboy* and everything else—hat sales were increasing. The timing was perfect. I got Stetson to guarantee enough sponsorship money that I got a meeting with Madison Square Garden. Al Grant was vice president, and he and I hit it off. He used to be with the Ice Capades; he understood a traveling show and everything that came with it.

"Al Grant was one of the smartest, nicest guys I think I've ever met in my life. He became a very big ally of mine. Here I was, a green kid, twenty-eight or twenty-nine years old, and this guy is someone I went to for advice. He would help me. That was the type of relationship we had. I relied on that guy for years. He was probably the most respected family-show promoter in the United States."

Gander was thirty years old the first time he produced a rodeo inside the historic confines of Madison Square Garden. He leaned on his ignorance and used it as a strength, and it was paying off.

"I wasn't arrogant; I was just dumb and dumb enough to ask people what to do," he said. "Just like my relationship with Al Grant: I learned early on that successful people are willing to share their success, expertise, and knowledge."

While the relationship was blossoming, they reached an agreement that enabled them both to succeed with World's Toughest Rodeo in the most iconic sports arena in the United States. With Stetson providing seed money to help underwrite the rodeo inside Madison Square Garden, Gander approached Grant with a proposal.

"When I first got there, I said, 'Is there some way you guys can be partners with me and do this together as long as Stetson's got enough seed money that you guys are partially protected?'" Gander said. "We met with some of their people and came up with a co-promotion deal, and I didn't even know what co-promotion was until then."

Gander quickly learned the importance of it and estimated that 50 to 60 percent of his agreements with buildings were co-promoted after that. Both sides had skin in the game, and it added up to a beneficial investment for producer and arena to team together. Still, there were some things everyone had to consider. There were several challenges to having a Western sports event inside Madison Square Garden, and Gander weaved his magic to make it happen five times between 1980 and 1992. He also counseled the PBR in the mid-2000s when the organization decided to go to the historic arena.

To unload dirt, panels, livestock, and all the other necessities to produce a rodeo, trucks backed their trailers into the bottom of the complex where the dock was in place. Manhattan isn't exactly a friendly place to drive, especially for semi-tractors hauling long trailers.

"Our trucks had to back through the door, and to do that, we had to go the wrong way down a one-way street," he said. "To do that, I had to buy off the cops around there. I had a pocket full of rodeo tickets for them, and that's how we got our stock into the building."

The other issue was finding appropriate dirt. Manhattan was built on a rock, so there wasn't any soil to be found on the island. Instead, Gander worked with others to obtain dirt from nearby New Jersey. The dirt had to be stored under the Brooklyn Bridge. When it was time to move into the building, small trucks had to navigate from the bridge to the Garden and up five stories using the ramps that were in place inside the complex. It was a similar system to making sure the panels and livestock were delivered to the arena floor—five flights up from the loading dock.

Over the years that he produced events in Madison Square Garden, Gander learned to juggle whatever challenges faced him. It wasn't just bribing New York City's finest; it was also marketing his product and selling tickets to potential buyers whose only knowledge of the Western way of life was on TV or at the movies. Still, there were other headaches he'd never imagined while growing up in the rural Midwest: labor unions.

"The big one was the spotlight operators; one was theatrical, and one was for sports," he said. "So, if we did an American opening with the national anthem and we wanted to spotlight the flag, that took a different union than the spotlight operators who were going to spotlight a cowboy when he was done with his ride. I decided to cancel the spotlight for the rides and just went with the theatrical operators. At that point, though, you're basically paying somebody to sit around.

"Another situation came up when we were unloading our trucks. It took the carpenters union to unstrap the bucking chutes and then it took the stagehands union to unload the bucking chutes. The stagehands who were unloading the chutes got the call a half hour earlier than the carpenters union that needed to unstrap the chutes, so you had the guys from one union standing around getting paid for half an hour while they were waiting for the guys from the other union to take the straps off the chutes.

"It just seemed like a waste of time and resources to me."

It was, but it was an early lesson he'd have to consider as he built his operation. Being in major markets was important to Gander, but that meant swerving around one obstacle to head directly into another. While they were barricades, they were also building blocks. Each instance straightened a vital learning curve as he continued to mold his product into a work of Western design.

Ask any artist—what they see in their mind's eye at the beginning of a project is vastly different than what the final piece will be. They capture the subject not just through color and line, but through restraint—letting blank space and darkness frame the light. Steve Gander's approach to building his brand is similar to this layering of paint—it's the undertones that create depth and authenticity.

Gander paid close attention to current events, and he learned of a sticky situation occurring in the Big Apple. New York City obtains its water from New Jersey, and in advance of World's Toughest Rodeo at Madison Square Garden, Gander noticed via news stories that New Jersey was threatening to control the amount of water supplied to New York. His mind raced before he made a phone call to Bobby Goldwater, who was handling public relations at the Garden.

"We already had Indian hoop dancers from the Alabama-Coushatta tribe from east Texas scheduled to come," Gander said. "I told Bobby, 'We could have the Indians do a rain dance for you guys to get rain.' Bobby thought it was a great idea. We had them come up a day early, but LaGuardia Airport wouldn't let them land because there were noise restrictions, and it was after midnight, so they were diverted to New Jersey. In the middle of the night, I called Bobby and said, 'I don't have any way of getting these guys to Central Park in time,' so Bobby sent Madison Square Garden's limousine to Newark, New Jersey, to pick up the Indians. They were late and literally changed their clothes in the limousine to do a rain dance in Central Park."

Whether it was a rain dance or not, it worked. The Native American boys did their best to put on a show for the crowd that had gathered, including several media outlets inspired to cover the stunt.

"That night it rained. It didn't rain very much, but it rained, and we got all kinds of publicity and had 54,000 people show up for the rodeo," Gander said. "Publicity makes your advertising believable."

CHAPTER 8

# PRELUDE: BUILDING A TEAM AND A BUSINESS

No successful man stands alone on an island. Individualism is where dreams die. That stationary plot of land is ravaged by waves of doubt, isolation, and contempt.

Steve Gander understood that well, and it was the bedrock of his business.

"No one is a self-made man," Gander said. "Every successful individual had a mentor or mentors. Successful business is the result of competent management or ownership's ability to attract and support the right people to work as a team. Much of my success can be attributed to having attracted hardworking, talented people who bought into my production and marketing concepts, and they contributed by making my ideas better.

"It is indisputable that the journey with my World's Toughest Rodeo family of coworkers made a positive impact on the rodeo industry. Our marketing, production, and business plans were revolutionary. What we were doing in the early 1980s is standard operating procedure in today's rodeo industry: video replay, open pageants, closing finale, staff meetings, production outlines, and musical overtures."

Those things came about because the team Gander built was influenced by creativity, perseverance, and an understanding that brainstorming ideas works in a group setting. World's Toughest Rodeo was managed democratically: Gander held 51 percent of the vote; the staff held 49 percent. The staff seemed to win more arguments, though, "because they were usually right; I was blessed they had the confidence to disagree with me."

While disagreements can spark volatile debate, the exchanges were meant to develop greatness. It's why Gander and his crew found prosperity with innovative measures meant to help fans interact with the action in the arena.

"My crew taught me empathy," he said. "I also learned I could win an argument but still find myself sleeping on the couch.

"My heroes are the good people who helped build World's Toughest Rodeo. They motivated me. Their genius kept me humble. We had fun overcoming challenges. I hope it was as good for them as they were to me."

The crew also learned a few lessons along the way. Kerri Allardyce was hired as a contemporary photographer. She was the first to shoot rodeo with a digital camera, which appealed to Gander and his wife, Peggy. Allardyce joined the World's Toughest Rodeo family in that capacity, but as she learned personally, the boss was always able to put willing folks in roles outside of the scope of their original posts.

Allardyce took over the media relations—preparing releases to submit to media outlets ahead of World's Toughest Rodeo's arrival in town. The stories were more of a cookie-cutter format where certain things were changed for each venue, and each stop had different offerings to entice ticket buyers. That's where due diligence can be handy, and it's where Allardyce learned one of her biggest lessons in the profession prior to an event in Madison, Wisconsin.

"In one of my press releases, I made an error," she said. "Where it was supposed to say, 'If you buy your tickets, kids get a free cowboy hat,' or something to that effect, I wrote, 'Kids are free.'"

Complimentary cowboy hats are one thing; free admission is another. She received a call from someone in Madison about the incorrect release while she was in the state's capital city. Allardyce flipped on the radio and heard the announcer make the statement she'd dreaded—that children would be admitted without charge.

"I veered off the road," Allardyce said. "I thought, 'Steve's going to kill me.' I was panicking. I called Peggy, and she was riding with Steve as they were driving to Madison. I was whispering to Peggy because I didn't want Steve to hear what I had to say. Finally, she said, 'Spit it out, Kerri.'

"I told her I really messed up, and I was almost crying. Steve could hear me because he was driving the truck, and Peggy was trying to stifle her laughter. Steve could be very stern and strict, and we'd all been put on notice because he had high expectations. I just knew I was getting fired or that I would have to pay for all these free kids' tickets out of my pocket. I was freaking out."

Gander listened to Allardyce's hysteria before asking the young phenom what she had intended to do to remedy the situation. She came up with the plan of action that was necessary—contacting the radio station to stop that promotion. She also updated the news release and re-submitted it to the media. Still, she had time to fret about the episode.

"When he walked into the arena, I was thinking he was going to kill me and fire me on the spot," Allardyce said.

Instead, "He said, 'What did you learn?' I go, 'Double-check press releases,' and he said, 'You won't make that mistake again, will you?'

"I was shocked, and then I started breathing again, but it was probably one of those things where he was laughing about it the whole time. I was making a way bigger deal out of it than it was. He was so cool, calm, and collected, and it made me appreciate him even more."

Allardyce was in her early 20s when that situation arose. She was still learning about herself, her photography, her approach to business, and how to overcome future challenges.

"In hindsight, he was laughing and giggling but was definitely stern," she said of Gander. "He held my feet to the fire and let me ride it out because the lesson was that when you do something painful, you'll never do it again. He was always kind and respectful and professional, yet warm and friendly and personable like a father figure.

"That wasn't just because I lived in the house with him and Peggy during the season. It's because that's who Steve is. He's very inviting and will have you sit down and ask you to a drink or show you the ranch. I had a very friendly, personable bond with him, but I also knew we were there to do a job."

Many who worked with Gander have continued to be part of rodeo, and most have thrived. The lessons they learned decades ago continue to impact how they go about their businesses and serve as a reason why they have taken the right steps to have a stable lifestyle in a sport based on the Old West.

"In my opinion, Steve Gander is the Wall Street of professional rodeo," said Roger Mooney, a longtime member of the World's Toughest Rodeo team and a nine-time NFR announcer (as of 2025). He has lent his voice to many of the top rodeos in North America. "He knew which buildings to rent and which to partner with. He knew the marketplace. He knew that television, radio time, and Madison Square Garden were expensive.

"He did it all with his own money, and Steve showed that no one in the history of rodeo has done it better."

While he's on a long list of dignitaries who have played a significant role in rodeo's place in Americana, Gander's style is what sticks out most to those who worked with him and those who continue to admire him.

"The very best piece of advice he ever gave me—and it's something I use every week—is, 'If you make everybody else look good, then you'll look good,'" Mooney said. "That was his slogan for his announcers, and I just took to it like a duck takes to water and incorporated it. You can be a show dog in the rodeo business when the spotlight hits you, but if you make everybody else look good, you'll look good, and the product will be good.

"I think the thing that exemplifies not only his work ethic but also his approach to the whole production is that he cared about what the ushers were doing because those were the people who met the faces of his audience."

In more than twenty-five years as the owner of World's Toughest Rodeo, Gander worked with dozens of rodeo professionals, some of whom have been recognized as elite in their respective careers.

"Our crew took tremendous pride in their work and made me look good," Gander said. "While I hope I haven't omitted any names, I have a list of people who were part of my crew, my heroes."

## PERSONNEL

Allardyce, Kerri
Banes, Shari
Bennen, Rhoda
Berry, Darrel
Brown, Johnny
Burlingame, Ray
Burns, Hal
Bush, TL
Chadwick, Jeff
Chadwick, Paul
Clark, TJ
Copeland, Jack
Copeland, Ruth
Cordiner, DC
Dermody, Dave
Dorenkamp, Jeff
Dorenkamp, Jerry
Dove, Cody
Ehert, Gwendy
Franzen, Brian
Gallano, John
Gander, Peggy
Myers, Kathi
Good, Allen
Kite-Good, Beth
Grolmus, Joel
Gwatney John
Gwatney, Sandy
Harrison, Carla
Heartsil, Tonch
Hiner, Troy
Honeycut, Scott
Hopp, Marcia
Horton, Chris
Hughes, Cory
Kemmit, Laurie
Kite, Chuck
Korkow, Jim
Korkow, TJ
Kreitz, Bob
Lahey, Kevin
Latting, Mike
Latting, Thyrl
Lucia, Tommy Joe
Marshall, Juma
Schultz, Mindy
Morehead, Angie
Rempelos, Steve
Morehead, Cory
Morehead, Courtney
Morehead, David
Morehead, Jake
Morehead, Lindsey
Morehead, Marla
Myer, Ben
Nevels, Allen
Nicolaus, Ruth
O'Connell, Ray
Parker, Jim
Pierson, Stu
Pilhofer, Gigi
Pilhofer, Nancy
Polhamus, Josh
Preacher Paul
Pullman, Bret
Fass, Cindy
Gentry, JimiBeth
Kurt, Jerry
Kurt, Jerry
Rempelos, John
Robinson, Jerome
Robinson, Tyler
Keldibeck, Rohat
Rustad, Rochelle
Sherwood, Kirk
Sikula, Mickey
Spraggins, Randy
Yerigan, Garrett
Steffen, Marrily
Steffen, Randy
Stiles, Butch
Thomas, Chip
Thomas, John
Thomas, Shane
Vadja, Zoli
Weaver, Debra
Weber, Nicki
Welch, Jacole
Wheelock, Bill
Widmer, Sharon
Yellowhawk, Daniel

## SPECIALTY PERSONNEL

Adams, Leon & Vicki
Barrett, Hadley
Bear, Morris
Bell, Zep
Brackett, Shawn
Bruce, Vince
Berry-Check, Beth
Check, Craig
Copeland, Dave
Corley, Randy
Crawford, DeDe
Davis, Bert
Diefenbach, Darrel
Dove, Zoop
Duba, Dusty
Eby, Ben
Fuller, Texas Jack
Fuller, Tim
Gines, Colby
Gratney, Rick
Harrison, John
Harter, Mike
Hodges, Robbie
Iodice, Angelo
Isley, Keith
Landis, Donnie
Lerwell, Troy
Lucia, Anthony
Lucia, Tommy
Mack, Jimmy
Martins, Marty
McAneny, Bill
McLain, Jim
McCracken, Gizmo
Meeks, Rory
Bishop-Minor, Tara
Mooney, Roger
Moorhead, Allen
Murry, Harold & Linda
Olson, Jerry Wayne & Judy
Olson, Allan
Orman, Lori Jo
Partlow, Ron
Payne, John
Payne, Lynn
Peters, Duane & Rose
Reid, Bobby
Rice and Renee
Rodriquez, Ryan
Reynolds, Max
Smets, Rob
Smith, Frankie "Punkintown"
Stevens, Tavia
Stewart, Andy
Stoker, J W
Swingler, Mark
Tallman, Bob
Thorton, Jerry
Throckmorton, Charlie
Tuckness, Timber
Turvey, Tommy
Tyer, Vicki
Ulmer, Mike
Yates, Hollywood
Lucia, Tommy Joe

## STOCK CONTRACTORS
4L Rodeo (C Lowrey)
Bar T Rodeo
Burkholder Rodeo (Donnie)
Burns Rodeo (Hal & Pete)
Classic Pro Rodeo (Scotty)
Cowtown Rodeo (Harris)
Dorenkamp Rodeo (Fred)
Franklin Rodeo
Gay, Neil
Growney, John
Hall, Del
Heartsil, Tonch
Honeycutt Rodeo (Roy)
Huntsel, Don
Korkow Rodeo (Jim)
Latting Rodeo (Thryl)
Mid-States (Johnny Walters)
Sears, James
Simon, Joe
Smith Pro Rodeo (Stace)
Three Hills (David)
Treadway Rodeo
Vold Rodeo (Harry)
Western Trails (Jerome)
Zinser (Jim & Maggie)

CHAPTER 9

# FINDING THE RIGHT PEOPLE

For most, rodeo is a brand of entertainment—a show that features a wondrous form of Americana and a taste of simpler times. It's a nod to the Old West and a fascination with cowboys and pioneers. Whether they're in the mountains of Colorado or on the shores of the Delaware River in Pilesgrove, New Jersey, the folks who attend events want to be captivated by the display before them.

They don't want to ride a bucking bronc or wrestle a steer; they want to imagine and smile, laugh at the clown, and enjoy the thrills and spills that come with the show. Rodeo fans will relish in the spectacle of the action before them while tolerating the smell of horse shit and moist dirt that fills the air.

It was Steve Gander's job to entertain them all, from the tiniest of tots to the oldest of old men, which is why he developed World's Toughest Rodeo. He knew the opportunity was there because of his experiences in rural America. He was raised in agriculture and toiled in the muck and mud on the family farm. He knew what odors lingered and what a long day in the field felt like.

Just like his father before him, Gander knew that in order to be successful, he had to build a solid team around him. While farming success relied heavily on Earl and Jean Gander and their children, World's Toughest needed folks who understood the ins and outs of the rodeo world. Whereas Earl Gander trained his crew by raising them, his eldest son knew he needed more expert care.

Enter Kathi Myers.

Raised in neighboring Illinois, Myers followed her daddy into rodeo. Eldon Spencer ran Lightning 4 Rodeo Productions, and not only did his daughter tag along, she became an integral part of the family business. She was a competitor, a barrel racer who ran fast horses around empty, 55-gallon drums that were set up to create a cloverleaf pattern. Barrel racing was developed in the early 20$^{th}$ century as an extension of trick-riding performances, eventually becoming a contest that transitioned into a timed event. It's been a natural fit in rodeo for decades.

So is Myers, which is why she became Gander's first employee so many years ago.

"This is really all I've ever done since the time I was thirteen, when dad bought into the rodeo company, and I started going with him during the summers," said Myers, a former president of the Women's Professional Rodeo Association (WPRA) who lives in New Jersey with her second husband, Jimmy. "I was just carrying flags and doing other things, and I started timing when I was like fifteen. I also started writing the contracts with the rodeos when I was a kid . . . I was really young when I started doing that stuff."

Eldon Spencer was just fifty-three years old when he died in 1971, but the lessons he passed on to his daughter remain apparent. From the hamlet of Port Byron, Illinois, near the Mississippi River, Myers took a post at her hometown exhibition, the Rock Island County Fair in East Moline, Illinois, where she not only built her resume but also continued to lay a foundation around an agriculture-based exposition and rodeo.

"My dad started that rodeo, so, intentionally, as I got older, I went to work for the fair association," she said. "Steve came to the rodeo over there and stopped in to say hi to me in the fair office."

It was more than just a chance meeting. Gander knew of Myers, a recent divorcee with two young children. He knew there was something underneath that exterior that was needed for World's Toughest Rodeo. During that conversation, he asked Myers what it would take for her to leave the fairgrounds and work for Gander.

"I remember saying, 'Probably not too much,' that if he were to pay me what I was making there, I'd be in. It happened just like that. As soon as the fair was over and I closed it out, I was looking for a place in Williamsburg to live."

It's just ninety-two miles from Port Byron to Williamsburg, Iowa, but she was venturing into untested territory. World's Toughest Rodeo was a start-up business, and while Gander's brilliant mind focused on what it was going to take to make everything work as he envisioned, Myers was leaving on an adventure of the unknown.

"I hired her because she knew more about rodeo than I did," Gander said. "She was a rodeo secretary. She just knew everything, and I was impressed with her personally, so I hired her as my first employee. We worked well together. We developed a bond that has stayed with us to this day. She remains a very dear friend."

Their connection was forged by rodeo. For those closest to it, passion drives them. The wealth, at first, is not fiscal; it's in the relationships they develop and the familial understanding that comes with the traveling road show. It's not just turning fast horses around barrels or riding wild bulls that were bred for athleticism and bucking style—it's understanding all that goes into being involved in the sport.

The way contestants view the sport is much different than the livestock producers who raise the bucking animals and timed-event cattle. The stock contractors see the game much differently than the event managers that produce the performances and the competition—and few, if any, can see each show the way that the audience does.

That's where Gander's genius comes in. He considered his moves based on the fans and their experiences at the rodeos he promoted and presented. He'd taken the time to study the people in the audience, how they parked, how they maneuvered around the complex, what they purchased at the concessions stands.

Gander was establishing something nobody had ever done before in the way he was doing it. He relied on good people, and they relied on him. The give-and-take was something that paid dividends, not just for World's Toughest Rodeo, but for the fans who enjoyed the shows.

"Steve's foresight was amazing," Myers said. "Once he decided he was going to do World's Toughest, he looked ahead at how it needed to grow and what he wanted to do with it, and he made it happen."

Like how Myers found her rodeo passion through family experience, Tommy Joe Lucia followed in the footsteps of his Hall of Fame father, Tommy Lucia, a well-recognized entertainer who may have been best known for his performances with Whiplash the Cowboy Monkey.

Tommy Joe Lucia paid for his college education through rodeo. He was a clown and entertainer, and though he had zero interest in pursuing a life in the sport like his father, he knew it was a perfect avenue to move toward the next big thing. Little did he know that he'd still be doing it decades later.

"When I graduated from college, I went up and clowned at some of Steve's events," Lucia said. He is the executive director of the Utah Days of '47 Rodeo in Salt Lake City and owner of Piranha Productions, a company that does event coordination, video screens, and provides other services for many rodeos across the country.

"I performed at some of Steve's events, and we started some discussions about me working for him at World's Toughest Rodeo.

"He hired me, and I moved my family to Iowa. I worked under Steve's direction in his office in Williamsburg. I was basically learning the ropes, mainly handling the production of the events, all of the operations, and logistics. Steve was the first to bring in dirt and put it on top of ice-skating and hockey rinks and navigate the waters of bringing the Western lifestyle into urban settings, specifically the Midwest and the Northeast."

It was groundbreaking, and others have followed the trail cut by Gander. The Professional Bull Riders (PBR) organization has major events in St. Louis; Manchester, New Hampshire; Albany, New York; and, of course, Madison Square Garden in New York City, to name a few. The PBR was established in the early 1990s, but Gander was putting on similar events in similar cities a decade before.

"I loved it," Lucia said. "I learned a lot from Steve, not only on the operation side and production side, but probably more importantly, the marketing and branding side. Steve is an expert, one of the originals in understanding how to brand. His branding with World's Toughest Rodeo was amazing. Some of the things they write, the current marketing books, it was just instinctively done by Steve, and that's why he was so successful."

Gander didn't just have a vision and a plan—he had the foresight to pass his knowledge on to others. Lucia still runs with many of the things he learned during his stint in Iowa. Steve Rempelos does, too.

Rempelos began his affiliation with World's Toughest Rodeo literally tooting his own horn. He was a trumpet player who performed in bands that played background music at rodeos, and by the early 1980s, Rempelos was leading his own ensemble. A recent graduate of North Texas State University (now the University of North Texas), he had ventured out into familiar territory on the rodeo trail, which is how he met Gander.

"I first met Steve in 1978 at the Minneapolis rodeo at the Met Center," Rempelos said. "Steve had ten rodeos, and I signed up for all of those events, pulling together the local guys for the band and working the shows. Being on the road was expensive, especially in those days, so I was not making a whole lot of money. Steve said that if I wanted to help, I could help set up and tear down the arenas, and he'd pick up my hotel room for the week.

"Three or four rodeos into the season, I helped out on a couple of radio remotes and those kinds of things, and Steve liked the way I helped out, so he offered me a position. That was in the spring, and I stayed out there for two or three years."

The band leader became a marketing assistant and worked closely with well-seasoned marketing veterans. That allowed Rempelos the opportunity to learn on the job while also following the path he'd set for himself making music.

"It was fun to be able to work and learn right out of college from some seasoned pros and, in Steve's case, directly from him," Rempelos said of Gander. "Steve is really caring on a personal level, and in those days, he was passionate and emotional at times. It always seemed to be underfunded like so many small businesses, but he was willing to give it his all both personally and financially in order to try to achieve some goals he had set. His passion really carried him through his creativity."

Just as he did with everything, Gander paid attention to all the things outside the original scope. Sure, Rempelos was a talented musician, but Gander observed there was much more to Rempelos' personality and demeanor. There was something deeper there that could be beneficial, not only to Gander's business model but also to Rempelos' future.

He is now the president and CEO of Starsports Inc., and the former chief marketing officer for the PRCA, the premier sanctioning body of the sport.

"Steve was very good with people," Gander said of Rempelos. "He was friends with everybody, very charismatic. Great guy to be around. He was a lot of fun and had a great work ethic."

One day over breakfast in St. Joseph, Missouri, Gander asked Rempelos if he wanted to be a marketing person.

Gander remembers Rempelos saying he didn't know anything about marketing. Gander told him, "You don't have to know anything about marketing. What you've got is a great work ethic and a good personality. I can teach you marketing, but I can't teach you work ethic."

"That's how we got to working together," Rempelos said.

The experiences Rempelos gained through Gander's tutelage paid dividends over the course of his career.

"All the basics of the event business have stuck with me over the years," the musician-turned-marketer said. "Working with Steve in that environment, I learned how to multitask, work hard, and certainly be aggressive in my jobs and positions."

Not everyone on the payroll came with exclusive work experience. Carla Harrison was a senior at California Polytechnic State University in San Luis Obispo, and she was looking for an internship to obtain her bachelor's degree. She was focused on doing something in agriculture communications and was told to contact Tommy Joe Lucia.

"I hadn't met Tommy Joe at the time, but he told me on the phone, 'Hey, if you want to learn from the best in marketing, you've got to go work for Steve Gander,'" Harrison said.

She interviewed with a few people before Steve Gander said, "I'd like to interview you."

"He called me at 7 a.m. Iowa time, which was 5 a.m. in California. I got up at 4:30, got the sleep out of my voice and interviewed with him. At the end of the interview, he said, 'I'd like to have you out to Iowa.' I went out there in late May or early June, and I stayed through the summer just to get acclimated there."

That was 2002, and World's Toughest Rodeo's season began in late fall, closing out its schedule in the spring of the following year.

"The girl who was there before me left, and she had been in media marketing," Harrison said. "He knew I was on an internship, but he literally just threw me into the fire, which was really such a good way to learn while knowing I had Steve there to back me up the whole time. At the same time, I also had Clay Galliard, who was great at marketing, so I had a pretty good safety net with people who knew what they were doing.

"I learned way more doing that than I ever could have learned out of a textbook."

So, Gander was a brilliant teacher, too?

"The things I love the most about Steve are his promotion, ability to sell something, break something down, repack it verbally, mentally, and resell it," she said. "I loved how he could make ushers feel like the most important people and do that with anybody he'd see at the rodeo, including the cowboys.

"He would talk to the ushers before every rodeo and tell them how important they were to our production because they were the first people that someone saw when they came through the door and if they had a problem, they were going to go to the usher. Steve's layers go on forever, and I think that's probably one of his strongest attributes. There's so much to learn from him. I just never get tired of being around him. When Steve talks, I shut up."

That's still the case today, decades since her internship. The lessons didn't stop when she earned her degree from Cal-Poly. Her roles have changed. Long married to a world-class rodeo entertainer John Harrison, she is the matriarch of the Clown Family and everything that comes with it.

The Harrisons own One Stop Shoppe Liquor in Hugo, Oklahoma, Harrison Real Estate, Kelly Bend Ranch, and Harrison Entertainment. Carla manages twenty-three rentals and other investment properties, helps at the liquor store, works with cattle, and assists with her husband's act when he's performing. Oh, and she's an auctioneer. Those hands-on marketing lessons she gained in the early 2000s remain an integral piece of her everyday life; one she shares with John and their four children.

Her husband was a trick and Roman rider when he first came into contact with Gander. From southeastern Oklahoma, John Harrison was trying to put together a resume as a specialty act. World's Toughest Rodeo needed something like that to help reach audiences and to trigger a bit of the Old West Shows along with bronc riding and barrel racing.

"John is extremely hard-working, honest, dedicated, and he's a good father," Gander said. "He's very good at what he does and is always trying to get better. He was pretty young when he started with us. I think John's done very well despite our influence."

That was a bit of comedy from the boss man, but Gander saw something in Harrison that he continues to see in the entertainer's work today.

"He has the characteristics of what you want a professional to be," Gander said.

By 2025, John Harrison had become one of the most recognized and award-winning entertainers in professional rodeo. He had been named the PRCA's Clown of the Year, Comedy Act of the Year, and Coors Man in the Can. He had been selected as the NFR barrelman ten times, but his legacy at ProRodeo's grand championship dates back to before he was even born.

His grandfather, Freckles Brown, was the 1962 world champion bull rider who conquered the "unrideable" Tornado in 1967 at the age of forty-six. The bull, owned by rodeo legend Jim Shoulders, had bucked 200 times without anyone lasting eight seconds until that December night in Oklahoma City.

With his family's legacy in place, John Harrison set out to do his own thing in rodeo. He began doing tricks while riding fast horses, then amped it up with Roman riding, whereby jockeys stand astride two horses galloping in unison. His expertise made for a showcase, which is why Gander hired him. Because Gander had already made a name for himself, it was a no-brainer for the Oklahoma man to head north and be part of World's Toughest Rodeo.

"When it comes to business, Steve Gander is one of the smartest guys I know who could take a company and build it from nothing to something that's worth millions," Harrison said. "He has the integrity that you want to work with. You know you're getting everything that he said and that there was nothing hidden.

"He was one of those guys that he hired you to do a job—if you do your job, you won't have any trouble. We never had any cross words. Steve's the type of person that if he had stern words to say, he didn't hold back. He would let you know what it was, but at five o'clock, a switch would come on, and he went from business mode to friend mode. Come the next day, it was back to business again. He was stern with his employees, but he kept it professional. That's something I've always respected about him."

Shortly after starting with World's Toughest Rodeo, John Harrison noticed a trend in the rodeo business. Fewer rodeos were hiring specialty acts, so the opportunities became more and more limited. That's when he changed his business model and became a rodeo clown with acts, but he added a bit of old-school flavor to his comedy. His trick riding became part of his schtick, and it's been a successful venture.

Some of that had to do with his upbringing and being around the sport his entire life. Some of that had to do with the people he's interacted with—people like Gander. Because of their time together, mostly at indoor events in the northern Midwest, Harrison has a better understanding of all aspects of the business side of rodeo.

"When we catch up now, it's fun to talk about all the time we were together, bring out stories," Harrison said. "I remember being in St. Paul, Minnesota, and performing before sold-out crowds, and he was as happy as can be. I also remember being in Dayton, Ohio, and it snowed like thirteen inches on the day of the performance. When the county shut the roads down, he didn't cancel the rodeo. He wasn't going to make any money; he was probably going to lose money, but he didn't come to us and ask us to take a lower check amount. He didn't try to talk our prices down. He paid us and thanked us.

"He's an upstanding man. His word is his word. He paid you what you agreed on, even if it meant he'd take a loss. That's the risk he takes, and hats off to him for doing that."

Some of the attributes that stick out most to people like John Harrison are Gander's work ethic and ability to work alongside people despite being a boss. If something needed to be done and nobody else was around, Gander did it—whether it was picking up trash or fitting panels together in the arena. It's what countless people saw.

David Morehead was pretty new to ProRodeo in the mid-1980s when he and Gander began working together. Their relationship has evolved ever since. Morehead and his family own Three Hills Rodeo based in Bernard, a community of 114 people in northeastern Iowa about eighteen miles from Dubuque. Gander needed a livestock contractor, and Morehead and his wife, Marla, fit in quite well.

"I got hooked up with Steve just out of bad luck," David Morehead said with a laugh. "Actually, that couldn't be further from the truth. I had gone to some of his events, and Steve had good enough faith in me to let me provide livestock for his World's Toughest Rodeo just after my first year in the PRCA. I was with him ever since. He had enough confidence in me to know that I was going to improve all the time. He was willing to go with me and give me enough business to have a viable company and stay afloat."

Three Hills Rodeo produces a dozen or so events a year and has livestock perform at several other major events across the country. Established in 1986, more than 500 animals call the Morehead ranch their home, and three generations of the family work together.

"Steve taught us basically everything we know about production and professionalism," Marla Morehead said. "It is something that has traveled on down the line to our grandkids. He always had a World's Toughest Rodeo personnel handbook, and the number one thing in that handbook was, 'You never get a second chance to make a first impression.'

"Those are the kinds of things that you learn from somebody who really has their foot on the accelerator. To do the right things, you have to have that kind of mentality."

It's why Gander found success with World's Toughest Rodeo. It's why Three Hills Rodeo has had success. In a profession where one source hires another most of the time, Gander wasn't just the promoter; he also was the underwriter who had to fund everything and hope that it all paid off in the end. When co-promotion with a venue was out of the question, Gander rented the buildings. Then he had to pay for all other aspects of the production, from bringing in contractors to making sure the dirt was just right.

He was the general of the operation; if there were some hiccups along the way, it all fell on Gander. He understood that part of the process, but he also leaned on other professionals to handle the business at hand. Every step was vital to find success, whether it was bringing smiles to a crowd or paying off the banker and showing a profit.

"Steve could be damned abrasive and even very demanding, but he was never unreasonable," David Morehead said. "As soon as you understood how to work with him and what he wanted, he was the easiest boss you could ever have.

"One of the things that sticks with you your entire career is just keeping things picked up. If you saw cup on the ground, you picked it up. It didn't matter if you threw it there or not. By association, you become creative and fussy about what you're presenting to the public. That's another thing that I got from Steve that I find priceless and hard to come by."

That's the attention to detail that Gander put into place decades ago. Gander sold World's Toughest Rodeo to Tommy Joe Lucia, who sold it to the Moreheads a few years later. The operation is now owned by Cinch Jeans and operated by Rorey Lemel, but the foundation remains.

David and Marla Morehead continue to rely on the Gander lessons they learned over their time with him. They can see the benefits of what it means to pay attention to the little things so the big things can work.

"Steve is a businessman," Marla said. "He's a production man. He's a bottom-line man. When at any time I got in a new building after we bought World's Toughest Rodeo, I always conferred with Steve, and he's so knowledgeable about so many aspects of the business that he's going to know. If it's the right place, if it's the right time, if it's the right move, he's the guy. He just has so much knowledge about all of the different aspects because he always spent his own money on it.

"He knew because he wasn't just out there working for somebody else, and I honestly think one of the biggest things he taught us is the amount of work it takes to make money using your own money. You can't just let everybody else do the work. You have to put your own sweat equity into the product if you're going to make it successful."

Hal Burns didn't know what to expect when he began working on the crew with World's Toughest Rodeo. It was the early 1990s, and Burns had been in rodeo most of his life.

"Steve Gander called and asked me if I'd like to go on their run," said Burns, a Wyoming cowboy who was part of Burns Rodeo and Summit Pro Rodeo. "At the time, I needed a winter job, and I said, 'Absolutely.' So, we loaded up and went to Madison Square Garden in New York City.

"I liked it enough. It was good. The crew was outstanding. The people that we were working with—the people that Steve had hired—were absolutely top-notch. We did an incredibly professional deal, and I really enjoyed those paychecks."

There weren't a lot of wintertime rodeos across the mountain states, so the opportunity for Burns was perfect. He could work in rodeo, showcase his own expertise, and still make a living. He was part of the livestock crew, so there was a lot to handle.

"When it comes to rodeos, Steve Gander is an absolute perfectionist," Burns said. "If you did things the way he wanted them done, he was good to work for. Dave Morehead and myself were partly on the livestock crew, so we worked a lot on the set-up and tear-down and had lots of meetings with him. I think that'd be the way you'd want to work with anybody; you just let me do my job, and if you like what I'm doing, we'll just keep doing it."

The work was good, and Burns realized that the Gander way was working. When things weren't right, Gander made sure the employees knew what needed to be better. Being a perfectionist isn't always about being right; it's about doing right, especially for those who purchased the tickets to be in those seats.

"I remember one time Steve thought we'd done a production that wasn't as good as it should have been, and in the staff room afterwards, he was pissed," Burns said. "He said, 'Everybody here is replaceable except that ticket-buyer, and that's who we work for.'

"I spent ten years on the PRCA Board of Directors, and I never forgot that. Steve took care of the ticket-buyers. To do that, he had to be meticulous and other things, but he understood who we were working for, and that was the person buying the ticket. He would go sit with the people in the grandstands and wait and look at the concessions lines and watch the whole thing just like anybody else that was sitting there.

"He would leave everything behind and go up and be part of the spectator crowd. That was something that really impressed me."

It's something, Burns said, that more producers and rodeo committees should look at doing. The organizers can learn a lot by sitting with the people who paid to be there. They can see the production from a different vantage point, and they can gain a better understanding of what the fans see when they make their way into the stands.

"That's what Steve was good at," Burns said. "That's what he did. The best thing I think he did was he took care of that ticket-buyer."

Some say success breeds contempt, that people who achieve goals will oftentimes drop their guards and become complacent in the day-to-day duties that got them to the top. That's never been the case with Steve Gander. He was driven, whether it was success at an individual rodeo or in his branding of World's Toughest Rodeo.

He managed people and partnerships. Sponsors weren't the only ones who reaped rewards from Gander's persona; he made sure his people found success, too. Behind every good leader are troops willing to outwork others.

Bob Kreitz retired in 1993 from Deluxe Corp., the Minneapolis-based company that prints checks. He was looking for something to fill his time. When World's Toughest Rodeo came to the Twin Cities the following winter, he signed up to help. He stayed at it for better than thirty years.

"In 1995, I would go to two or three rodeos with them," said Kreitz, still active in his 80s. "I worked the crew, set up chutes, tore down the chutes, and swept floors. I did whatever they needed. I was a labor contractor; I never rode, but I carried a (PRCA) rodeo labor card."

Kreitz was a jack-of-all-trades type for Gander. If something needed done, Kreitz was on top of it.

"Bob showed up at the back door of the rodeo one time and wanted a job, and I put him to work," Gander said. "He was a hard worker, and he made a great impression on the young guys who were working because he thought no job was too little. He was just a good influence on a number of guys. He had a great work ethic."

One of Gander's many impressions was this: "If you're too big for the little jobs, then you're not big enough to work for World's Toughest Rodeo." Kreitz set a good example of what that meant better than anyone.

That seemed to be a common theme for Gander as he continued to fill his team over the years. He had his experts, but he was also willing to put people in roles they did not originally sign up for. Call it foresight, call it intellect, or call it sheer luck, but it worked.

Every organization needs someone like Bob Kreitz.

"I would work fifteen rodeos every year for Steve," he said. "Some of them, if they were close, I drove to. I lived further north than anyone else. I was in St. Paul (Minnesota), and everyone else was in Iowa. Sometimes I drove myself or I flew there. Sometimes I drove to Cedar Rapids (Iowa) and rode with Rory Meeks in the chute truck or I'd go to Moreheads' ranch and ride with the stock trailer.

"I did anything Steve wanted me to. I told him if he could teach me how to do it, then I would do it."

In any hive, there are thousands of worker bees for every queen. They know their roles, and they can expand upon them as necessary. Similarly, at World's Toughest Rodeo, there was plenty of input from the staff and crew. Gander respected his team's input, and many of World's Toughest Rodeo's innovations came from his team.

"I was blessed to have good, dedicated people around me," Gander said. "They made the World's Toughest Rodeo brand shine when I was stressed. They often forgave me for being human. I learned from each of them. They made me a better manager and a better person."

"Steve was very good at management," Kreitz said. "A lot of people—who had nothing against him—would say, 'Well, he's kind of grouchy at rodeos.' I worked with all these different stock contractors when I wasn't working with him in the winters, and I noticed the same behavior from them.

"When the rodeo was on, he was business. Afterwards, he'd sit down and have a beer and a cigar with the crew. He was easy to work with, but when you're putting on something like a rodeo or business, you've got to maintain your business and worry about your play later. He did it that way."

Everyone who worked for World's Toughest Rodeo understood that. Steve Gander had a way of handling his business, and those that bought into it helped define success. When Keith Isley signed up to work some of the events, he wasn't quite as popular among rodeo fans as he eventually became.

Isley was still trying to make a name for himself. By the time he retired at the end of 2024, he was one of the most decorated funnymen in rodeo, but that wasn't the case when Gander hired him decades ago. The entertainer and clown had been working in the IPRA for several years and was breaking into the PRCA—World's Toughest Rodeo has been part of both organizations over the years.

"Keith was one of those guys that I'd heard about, and we hit it off immediately," Gander said. "He was an IRA guy long before, but I had not worked with him there. He was always very flexible, and to this day, I think he's one of the premier entertainers in the sport of rodeo.

"He learned a lot from Lecile Harris. Keith would work his acts for a year before putting them in a rodeo. He would work them on Saturday mornings with a clown or announcer, whomever he was working with. You can still see his influences on John Harrison, who might be the biggest name in rodeo entertainment today."

Over his career in the PRCA, Isley earned numerous honors in a span of two decades. He was named the Clown of the Year and the Coors Man in the Can [for the top barrelman] six times each, and he was a ten-time Specialty Act of the Year. That all came after his stint with World's Toughest Rodeo.

"Quite a few years ago out of the blue, Steve called me and wondered if I'd be interest in working the World's Toughest," Isley said. "I was excited about working for him because it was kind of a big deal. Two weeks later, he called me back and said he wasn't going to be able to make it work. I'm thinking, 'That's a short career with World's Toughest . . . just two weeks.'

"The next year, he called me back, and we finally agreed on the deal. His secretary called and said I needed to send them some pictures because they didn't even know what Keith Isley looked like. When she said that, it put an idea in my head."

Isley's sense of humor came into play almost immediately. It didn't take long before he had the right response to the situation.

"I was working some rodeos around home [in North Carolina]. There was a photographer that had a photograph of this biker dude in a tank top with tattoos on his arm, so I asked [the photographer] if I could have that photo. I got it and sent it to World's Toughest Rodeo and told them that this was the only photo I had of me on such short notice and that I hoped it worked out for them. I said, 'P.S., the people really liked the tattoo.'

"His secretary, Sharon, called me a few days later and said they really liked the photo, and they'd made copies and were going to make some autograph sheets for me to sign."

It was the perfect introduction for a man who made a living on comedy while also showcasing his athleticism and horsemanship skills gained in a lifetime of Western sports. Isley also gained a ton of respect for how the business of World's Toughest Rodeo was handled. When it came down to signing a contract, Isley took note of a few things in the document that weren't going to work. He mentioned them to Gander, who told the entertainer to just cross through what was wrong and sign the deal with those adjustments.

"The only time we ever had a contract was that first year, and after that, it was just a handshake deal," Isley said. "It was a lot like a family deal that involved some production. I could see some of the stuff Steve had done, and I was wondering, 'My God, what is this man thinking here?' But it worked for him. The ideas that he had might have been a little bit off the wall at times, but they sold tickets, and that's what it was about. You have to keep the people entertained.

"I learned a lot about production when I was with Steve. He went into some of these major cities, and they expected a performance. Given that it was World's Toughest Rodeo, that title there said something about the production end of the rodeo."

Entertainers are a valuable piece of the rodeo-production puzzle. Not only are they vital to helping add value to the show, they are imperative to the timing. Clowns like Isley thrived in the walk-and-talk, where the entertainers make observations throughout the show.

It's a great way to keep the crowds engaged between runs and rides, helping maintain a seamless transition. They work closely with announcers, who are prolific in engaging audiences. All came together with Gander to make sure the ticket-buyers got the best bang for their buck.

"I don't know what Steve's IQ is, but I'd say he's bumping on genius," said Roger Mooney, who started with World's Toughest Rodeo with Gander decades ago and still calls the action at many of the events today. "He was from Iowa and had that Midwestern work ethic. He was at the coliseum long before anybody else, and he was there long after everyone was gone.

"He strategized. He was working on January stuff in May, June, and July. He knew all the media, every television and radio interview. He was on top of everything that needed to be handled."

That sums up Steve Gander, and it's why his brand of entertainment remains successful decades after he began World's Toughest Rodeo.

CHAPTER 10

# THE GANDER APPROACH

Steve Gander was a master technician when it came to rodeo promotion. He understood the game—from a fan at first, to a contestant, then finally a man who set his own wheels in motion with the creation of World's Toughest Rodeo.

While they've become commonplace in rodeo, Gander's innovations in the 1980s set a standard. He offered replay video long before anyone ever considered doing so, even at the biggest events in the sport. The National Finals Rodeo—the world's biggest event that features only the elite cowboys and cowgirls in the game each year—didn't follow suit for decades.

"A lot of the buildings and arenas we were at were NBA and NHL buildings, so they had these big jumbotrons," Gander said. "People that came to those basketball games or anything else at those places were used to seeing large telescreens. One of the things we wanted was for the people in Cedar Rapids, Iowa, to have the same show that Minneapolis had, so we started carrying our own equipment just to upgrade our shows, and it was phenomenal.

"We would go into smaller markets and put those telescreens up, and spectators weren't used to having slow-motion replay on a giant screen. It really elevated us."

Gander's vision superseded what most could imagine at the time. From putting dirt on top of ice rinks to expedite his shows during hockey season, to producing a telecast of the event that gave ticket-buyers a better experience—most everything worked. World's Toughest Rodeo is still viable decades after it began because of the grandiose ideas Gander brought to the table.

"Steve had sponsorships and was able to develop things before this industry even knew how to do it," said Tommy Joe Lucia, who worked for Gander at World's Toughest Rodeo before purchasing the business years later. "He had packages that included media. Steve started doing broadcasts of rodeos, and it was the grassroots of raw broadcast rodeo. He would record his rodeos, and we were the ones to first bring big screens to the sport. It was a rear-projection, and those projectors weighed 350 pounds and cost $55,000. We had to get people in the seats and give them more than they expected. He wanted replay and video at all of his rodeos."

Gander gathered video of his rodeos, then put together a thirty-minute television infomercial. He also bought time on stations, then aired the broadcast in ways that were self-serving and educational.

"We see it now all the time, but back then, he was the real pioneer of all that," Lucia said.

"It was the easiest thing in the world," Gander said. "Back in the early '90s, there were a lot of commercials being put on TV, especially the independent stations. I just took the idea of creating a campaign that would be a combination of WWE and an infomercial for a vacuum cleaner and made a half-hour rodeo highlight reel for us. We had all of our promo locations in it for wherever our rodeo was going to be the following weekend.

"Sunday afternoon was our favorite time for commercials. That time of year, you had NBA basketball. We'd be on one of the networks competing against the NBA for viewers, and our ratings would beat NBA games consistently. We would take some of our promo schedule on TV to promote that the show was going to be on Sunday afternoon on Channel 9 in Minneapolis, so we had people looking forward to it. That's how we competed against the NBA."

Each Sunday featured a commercial for the upcoming location. One week it was Chicago, the next it was Cleveland, and so on, and that occurred for many years until buying commercial time became cost-inefficient. Instead, he found a combination of other ways to promote his product that got him more exposure.

"When I started producing rodeos, 60 to 70 percent of the budget for family shows like the circus were spent on newspaper, billboards, and posters," Gander said. "When I started, I was using 60 to 70 percent on television; my justification was that rodeo was visual and had action. The big difficulty that I had early was that I didn't have good footage.

"Much of my commercials were bull wrecks or if we were giving away free cowboy hats, then you saw kids in our commercial. We'd say, 'Free cowboy hats,' and you'd see a kid wearing a cowboy hat. That's what worked for us in the early '80s."

Lucia was with World's Toughest for several years, starting as an entertainer. He worked his way up, helping with event coordination, operations, and planning. He was building a resume that has equipped him with great success over the years, including a stint at the PBR, the premier association for stand-alone bull riding. When Gander put World's Toughest up for sale, Lucia purchased it and ran the operation for some time before selling it himself.

"Steve was the best boss I ever had—I'm not really good at working for anybody because I like to do it my way," Lucia said.

"For as long as I worked with Steve, he must have allowed me to do it my way, or I probably would have quit a long time before. I was learning so much from him. Because of my relationship with Steve, I built all the templates and current stuff that I do to produce everything from Indy Car Racing to the Days of '47 Rodeo."

Everything that happened with World's Toughest Rodeo since the late 1970s came about because Gander believed in what he was doing and where he was taking his product. He invested in it fully, taking out loans to cover his expenses with plans to repay the debts as quickly as possible. Everything was on his shoulders, but he wouldn't have it any other way. Gander always tried to hire the right people to make sure his dreams could become a reality.

"A lot of people would look at him and want what Steve Gander was doing and what he had; they just weren't willing to pay the price Steve was willing to pay," Roger Mooney said. "He paid the price."

Mooney's Georgia drawl is just part of his delivery, and it's one of the reasons why he had worked the NFR so many times. He has been part of rodeo production for better than thirty years and has a say in how things happen and when they happen, during every performance he calls.

"I started working with Steve as his second-string quarterback between Duane Peters, Hadley Barrett, Randy Corley, and some other guys he was using," Mooney said, referring to some of the great announcers in rodeo history. "I was working for Three Hills Rodeo and Dave Morehead, who was pretty much the stock contractor of choice for World's Toughest.

"It wasn't long before I was his first-string quarterback, and I've worked a quarter century for it."

Mooney's working relationship with Gander developed over time because they were after the same thing: what was best for the audience in attendance.

"Roger played an important role in our rodeo," Gander said. "Number one, he was flexible and teachable. He said what he needed to say. If I needed him to say what he wanted to say in fifteen seconds, he gave you fifteen seconds; if you wanted it done in five, it was five. A lot of the guys didn't take direction and weren't listening, but he listened better than anybody and worked very hard at it."

That went both ways. Communication is key in any relationship, but announcers must be able to relate to the men who write the checks, especially when it comes to the production. Mooney is more than an announcer. He is also a bit of an historian, someone who can speak about the event while also talking about the generations of athletes who came before, whether it's a third-generation steer wrestler from Oklahoma or a bucking mare with champion lineage.

"I learned more from Steve Gander than anybody else," Mooney said. "If you ever talked to anybody and they didn't like Steve Gander, it's probably just because he beat them to the punch. He was just so good in the arena that there hasn't been anybody better.

"He was a great guy to work for because of that."

Gander was critical of himself and others around him. He strived for greatness in himself and in the events he produced. He sought perfection as much as possible, and everyone who found success in World's Toughest Rodeo understood what it meant to make his or her best effort to find it.

"Steve was very demanding in the earlier years," Mooney said. "He might even invoke fear in some of the personnel, but in later years, he got a lot more laid back, a lot more friendly to the people that worked for him. They all came to like working for him, and he's a testament to what it's about in the rodeo producer industry. Unlike a lot of them, he didn't use somebody else's money."

Mooney saw virtually every side to Gander when it came to the rodeo business. They were together through some of the best times of World's Toughest Rodeo, and they experienced the rough moments, too. They also shared laughs and enjoyed a post-show cocktail or two.

"One of the greatest memories I have is when he really would do well at the box office and the product was good for the ticket-buyers, he would come by, grin, and would never look at me," Mooney said. "He would look straight ahead and say, 'You know, Roger, I'm going to keep you around until you get it right.' I would always look straight ahead, never look at him and say, 'We're good; I'm going to keep making mistakes, because that's job security.'

"We said that to each other for fifteen or twenty years."

There was also a time in St. Paul, Minnesota, when Gander approached his announcing protégé after a wondrously successful evening. He'd produced a double-header, one in Minnesota and one in Atlanta, and both venues sold out. When the night closed, Gander approached Mooney with a memory-maker.

"He lit up a cigar that I swear was twelve inches long; it looked like Boss Hogg from the *Dukes of Hazzard* TV show," Mooney said. "He broke the seal off a bottle of Jack Daniels and tossed that lid on the ground, which was very uncharacteristic of Gander because he was always on the crew, saying, 'If you see a piece of trash, you pick it up; I want my brand and my show to look good to everybody, whether you're six, sixty-six or ninety-six. We run a tight ship.'

"He tossed that lid, which told me one thing: It's not going back on until that bottle was gone. He said, 'I made more money tonight, Roger, than I've ever made.' He said it in a way that was still humble, and he had the uncanny ability to still be the lead dog, the tip of the sword, and the best there was ever to do what he did. Whether you liked Steve Gander or you didn't, you could sit back and look at him because he was the best going up and down the highway with what he'd done."

Rodeo is a humbling sport in its nature. Cowboys and cowgirls are not given any assured paychecks; they must beat most of the field to earn money, and they pay a fee in order to enter a competition. Most other professional athletes don't. Tom Brady's last NFL contract with the Tampa Bay Buccaneers paid him $50 million for two years. LeBron James earned more than $100 million for his two-year contract with the Los Angeles Lakers of the NBA from 2023-25. The teams also take care of all traveling expenses and medical costs.

If a cowboy bucks off or a barrel racer knocks over an empty, 55-gallon drum, he or she is out any chance at cashing in. A world championship is the most cherished title in rodeo, but the hoopla surrounding a gold buckle only lasts a few weeks. When the new season begins, every cowboy starts over.

It's the same for producers like Gander. While he may have enjoyed his most profitable night with his doubleheader in St. Paul and Atlanta, there were also nights and locations that didn't perform nearly as well. Mooney was with Gander at one of those stops.

"One time we were in the Ice Palace in Tampa (Florida), and we were the second event to ever happen in there," Mooney said. "The first night was opening night of hockey; the second night was us. It was a one-performance rodeo. The shrubs were not even plated outside the Ice Palace. I think Steve lost $70,000 to $75,000, but he walked to everybody, smiled, handed out the checks and said, 'Thank you.'

"Sure, that had to eat him up, but he never let the rest of us know it. It was never, 'Hey, I lost my hind end, so I've got to cut your pay this week,' or 'I need you to be my partner in this loss.'

"Steve was Wall Street—he took care of business."

It wasn't just the business of World's Toughest, though. Gander had a history of passing on his experiences to others. He wrote a book—*Rodeo Event Marketing: The Business of Getting B.I.T.S. (Butts In The Seats)*—in which he shared his thoughts, ideas, and decisions. He taught Steve Rempelos the importance of marketing and media; he showed Lucia the foundation to a great production; he helped Mooney tell a better story.

"Steve Gander is probably the best media-buyer of any person I've ever been around in my life," said John Gwatney, a former World's Toughest operations manager who is now a production coordinator for dozens of rodeos across the country and a major contributor to the NFR.

"When we bought media for that year, we'd go to those different towns and play 'Good Cop, Bad Cop.' I was basically the good cop. Steve would wear a business suit and didn't even show any cowboy in him. We would go into those places, and he would negotiate when he's going to get commercials and promotional spots at the best possible price. He knew how to negotiate and get major media deals.

"He taught me a little bit about that. Now, is that something I wanted to pursue? No, not really, but at least I know, and he opened my eyes to that stuff. He had a complete, well-rounded rodeo production company, and it was all on his back. He would hock his place for the run to have front money for that run of rodeos, and me being a silly cowboy that I am, I didn't realize that farmers do that for their crops, too."

Bankers want collateral before they'll offer an agriculture loan. Gander understood that aspect in rural America. Farmers need that front money to cover the cost of seed, materials, and diesel to get the crops in the ground. The loan may need to pay for operations until the harvest, when the ag producer can sell his grain and cover the debt and hopefully come out with a profit.

It was only fitting for Steve Gander to play his game with house money.

"Steve did that every year," Gwatney said. "He would borrow money, then he'd pay it back at the end of the run."

There was more to it, though. Gander wasn't just about his own well-being. Just as he offered tutelage to those that wanted it, Gander oftentimes looked out for those with whom he worked. He wanted good employees—the people he trusted his brand with the most. He made sure they had work when they needed it. He took care of them so they could help take care of his brand, his product.

"There were a couple of places we went that he did not make money, but he had the rodeo just so everyone on the staff was making money," Gwatney said. "There were a couple of those dives that we did regularly just so he could keep his crew working."

Gander's focused approach to business brought out the best in World's Toughest Rodeo and the people he had to help him produce each performance. He established his brand, then built it into a powerhouse. He gambled on himself, and before raking in the chips, he hinted to others at the same table how to best play the game.

*David Morehead (left) visits with World's Toughest Rodeo crewmates Tommy Joe Lucia (center) and Hal Burns during a 1996 event. Morehead worked with Gander for three decades before eventually owning the company for a few years.*

Steve Gander called this crew – from left, Rory Meeks, David Morehead, John Thomas, John Hamrick, and Chuck Kite – his A team and got this image of them in Dayton, Ohio.

*Steve Gander and his team of professionals took great pride in having the sport's cleanest and neatest arenas, even in the pens behind the chutes where the animals were kept.*

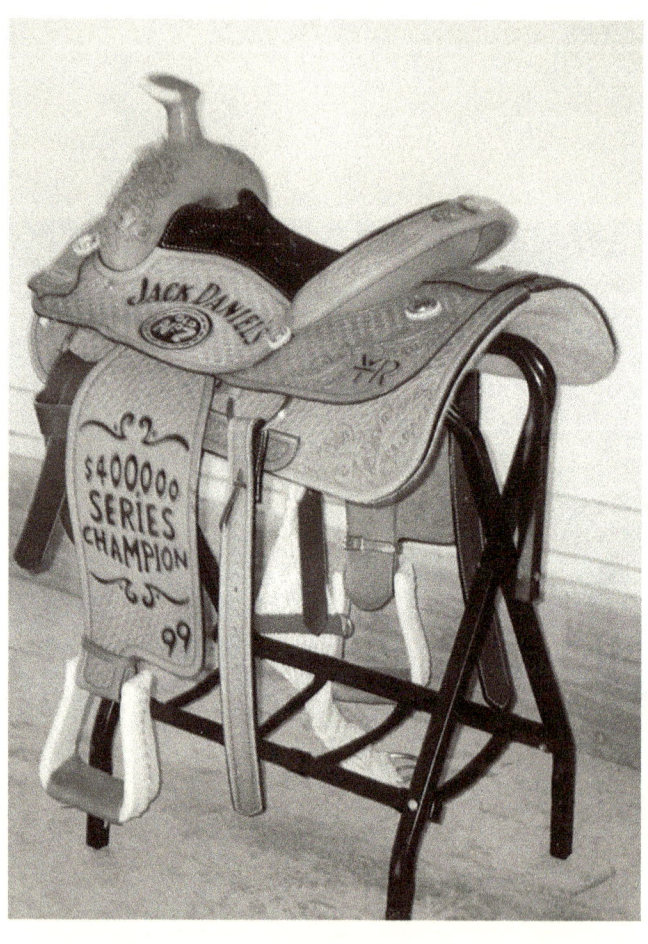

*Rodeo trophies are not only rewards but also items that can be used, like this 1999 championship saddle.*

*Steve Gander believed in pageantry at World's Toughest Rodeos, from instant replay on giant screens to music, sound effects, spotlights, and special introductions, including two bulls dubbed as the Demon Brothers.*

*Pickup man Mickey Sikula leads Dollor, the horse John Wayne rode in several movies, during a special tribute to Wayne at Madison Square Garden in 1981.*

*John Wayne rode Dollor during six of his movies, including "The Shootist," which was Wayne's final film. Steve Gander acquired 1,600-pound chestnut Quarter Horse to utilize during openings with a tribute to Wayne.*

*Sharon Widmer posts with Old Glory during the opening of a World's Toughest Rodeo in 1994 at Cedar Rapids, Iowa. Steve Gander and the team believed in having large flags for the national anthem.*

*Steve Gander plays on his family's place in northeastern Iowa when he was a young boy.*

*Steve Gander was oftentimes a traffic cop, helping ensure the behind-the-scenes work was done properly to help ticket-buyers enjoy their time at a World's Toughest Rodeo.*

*Steve Gander publicity shot*

*Gander near middle school age*

*Steve Gander poses while working at his home office in Williamsburg, Iowa, in 1980.*

*Gander senior photo*

*Peggy and Steve Gander stand before an officiant during their December 2000 wedding in Las Vegas.*

*Steve and Peggy Gander were guests of Gund Arena in Cleveland for an NBA game when basketball legend Michael Jordan came out of retirement for the Chicago Bulls in their game against the Cleveland Cavaliers.*

*Just as Steve Gander loved great openings to his events,
he also realized that many fans in attendance loved to watch bull riding,
which had long been considered the most popular event to watch.
That's why he had a special intro to the final event of each performance.*

One of Steve Gander's goals when he created World's Toughest Rodeo was to take the sport back to Madison Square Garden, possibly the most recognized arena in the world. He produced rodeos in that storied building several times.

*Steve Gander worked with an illusionist to create a magic act during some of his openings. He built a wagon for an act to make a horse appear in the middle of an arena filled with thousands of fans.*

In addition to owning World's Toughest Rodeo and Dodge Rodeo, Steve Gander also tried his hand at raising bucking animals, like the mares and colts in this image. His love for horses has continued over the years.

*Neal McCoy was one of several artists who performed concerts after World's Toughest Rodeos. McCoy was traveling with World's Toughest when "No Doubt About It" reached number one on the Country Music charts in 1994. McCoy (second from left) poses with (from left) Steve Gander, Rooster Kersten and Zoop Dove.*

*Trick riders carry a giant American flag in unison during their act at a World's Toughest Rodeo. Steve Gander believed it was important that every performance renewed patriotic ideals and pride in the country.*

*President Ronald Reagan addresses professional rodeo athletes and World's Toughest Rodeo personnel after the historic Command Performance Rodeo in 1983 at Landover, Maryland. A reception followed the rodeo later that day at the White House, where President Reagan again told attendees about the importance of cowboys (and cowgirls) to the history of the United States. (Photo by Jim Fain)*

*Steve Gander rides through a river near Eminence, Missouri. Termite was one of the horses he raised.*

*Ted Harbin*

*Steve Gander has had a passion for trail riding at historic places, including a 110-mile trek over seven days on his team roping horse, Twister, in 2005. He slept under the stars and rode across the Big Horn Mountains in Wyoming.*

CHAPTER 11

# MARKETING A DIFFERENT PRODUCT

By the late 1990s, Steve Gander's name was synonymous with rodeo excellence.

He'd built a brand with World's Toughest Rodeo and had taken the Old West into big cities in America—in major sports arenas. The productions had become legendary, as had Gander's approach to marketing a sport based on ranching traditions. He had ridden the ebbs and flows that come with live event promotion and came out on top.

Gander's formula was growing more mainstream in a sport that relied on history. More people in the cities were further from the farming and ranching lifestyles that had built the country, that had put food on tables for centuries. City-dwellers still flocked to the Gund Center in Cleveland and to Rosemont Horizon in Chicago for the spectacle of World's Toughest Rodeo.

As Gander's approach continued to gain momentum, his overall expertise was put on display. Being a promoter, producer, marketer, and the founding father of the rising commodity, many wanted to get everything they could out of the Iowa-born genius. That included folks involved with Dodge Rodeo, which was a marketing company centered around the Chrysler pickup truck brand.

"I started with Dodge before they were part of the PRCA," Gander said of the largest organization in the sport. "Dodge was trying to talk to the PRCA, and the PRCA wouldn't talk to them. I had a Dodge sponsorship at my rodeos for a whole year before they signed a deal with the PRCA."

Dodge Rodeo provided foundational marketing and went back to a dealer named Jack Lowry, who took pickups to horse shows and rodeos. He had the vehicles prepared with after-market features for sale at the events. Lowry's program helped him sell a lot of trucks, which caught the attention of Chrysler's executives.

"They wanted him to sell his dealership and start the program, and they pretty much gave him carte blanche to do whatever it took," Gander said. "It had been going on since 1980, and we knew it was a great program because it had dealer involvement. NASCAR doesn't really have dealer involvement—it's more of a national thing. The rodeo program goes to the grassroots, and the dealer has to make the commitment that he's going to help promote the local rodeo."

Lowry had built a stable business, and things were going well for Dodge Rodeo. But Lowry had been stricken with Parkinson's disease, a chronic neurodegenerative disorder that is progressive and affects movement, coordination, and balance. He was looking for a replacement before his illness worsened, so he and partner Jim Owen contacted Gander.

"They wanted me to buy the company," Gander said. "I told them, 'Well, I've got my hands full now—are you talking to anybody else?'"

The duo planned to talk to others about the prospect of buying Dodge Rodeo. With that in mind, Gander broached the subject while understanding what repercussions might be for the partnership that was already in place between Dodge and World's Toughest Rodeo.

"I said, 'Well, I'm not interested at this time,'" Gander recalled. "My concern is someone might end up with a company thinking that I was negotiating against them, and I could lose my sponsorship with Dodge. Am I willing to consider if no one else is at the table?"

That's exactly what happened. Lowry hadn't found any other appropriate takers after a few months had passed, so he called back to the Iowa phone number. With that, Gander took a flight to Atlanta and did his due diligence on all aspects of the company, spending three days doing so. By the time he was done on his venture, he was willing to purchase the company. Lowery, Owen, and Gander flew to Chrysler's headquarters in Detroit and gave their blessings on the sale.

"Jack mastered the program, and he lived and breathed it," Gander said. "In order for something to be successful, somebody has to have the passion and undying belief that this is the right way to do something. He knew trucks, he knew marketing, and he had the passion to go out and get it done."

Gander had a firm grasp of that concept. Passion is what drove him from an early age and what facilitated the incredible run he'd accomplished with World's Toughest. Now, Dodge Rodeo was in his lap, and he needed to caress it a bit to help elevate the product.

"The program was kind of stuck in not having an increase in sales, and I got an increase," he said. "I put together a multi-year contract between Chrysler and the PRCA, which I thought made for better marketing for Dodge and more security for the PRCA. We also did surveys with dealers to get their data and study it to see if we needed to be doing something different.

"Those surveys helped save the program on the humane issues, when the program was attacked at an annual shareholders' meeting questioning the $6 million rodeo program."

On the Friday of the long Memorial holiday weekend, a Chrysler executive called Gander, instructing Gander to justify the rodeo program in two pages or less by the following Tuesday. Gander spent an entire weekend perfecting his prose, and it saved the program. An executive called Gander and told him not to worry about the humane issue; Detroit would deal with it.

"We also made the Dodge Truck program for the stock contractors to receive a Dodge truck a little fairer and more equitable," Gander said. "Before I bought Dodge Rodeo, you received a truck because of where you lived or if you were on the PRCA board. We made it possible for whichever stock contractors had the most Dodge rodeos to get the trucks. If you had nine Dodge rodeos and everybody else had eight Dodge rodeos, you got first pick on a truck. We made the program fairer, and we got the budget increased.

"We also started sponsoring the steer roping finals. When I negotiated the first multi-year agreement between Dodge and the PRCA, we became the title sponsor of each circuit finals. It was the first agreement between the PRCA and Chrysler since 1992."

The program grew. The organization had twenty-nine employees and events in most states.

"We had a great crew," Gander said. "They represented Dodge and our company with professionalism. You could trust every one of them."

Gander had taken the reins in a seemingly comfortable way, but in reality, it was far from it. When he began World's Toughest Rodeo, everything involved was his baby, from the planning stages to the marketing to the final product. He set the procedure, initiated the first steps, and scheduled the media. He hired the right people from the onset and established an order. He knew that to make it work, he was going to have to build a product that would attract ticket-buyers and sponsors alike.

"When I had World's Toughest Rodeo, I was an entrepreneur and didn't really have to answer to anybody," Gander said. "The Dodge Rodeo program taught me that you might be the boss, but you still have to answer to somebody. I think that made me a little bit better when I was consulting with Mesquite Rodeo, Askarben, the PBR, and some of those other projects.

"I'm still a very dominating person in a meeting. I come to a meeting prepared, and if I think I'm right, you are not going to beat me in the discussion. You might get pissed off, but my job is to get you to buy into what I think needs to be done to benefit all parties."

Through meetings with Chrysler, he learned a little more about himself. He established himself and his marketing procedures, but he knew the final answer was going to be made by the folks in Detroit.

"Working with Chrysler was a really good experience, and I went through a couple different Chrysler ownerships," he said. "We had the humane issue to fight a couple of times, but as long as we did our homework and our job, it was a great company to work with."

Rodeo involves animals, and there are some entities that don't like it. Groups like People for the Ethical Treatment of Animals and Showing Animals Respect and Kindness have been adamant in their belief that rodeo is not in the best interest of the animals involved. They have lobbied against Western sports and other expositions that feature animals, creating a humane issue for producers of such shows.

Gander approached the discontent with the facts that surround Western sports—that the animals aren't mistreated in any regard and that they receive the utmost care along the way. That's what he presented to the bosses at Chrysler, and it's one of the reasons the company continued to support the program. In the mid-1980s, Gander was instrumental in getting the flank-strap law reversed in Ohio.

By the time Gander took the reins of Dodge Rodeo, Mike Orman had served as a field representative for the company for several years. He'd been to World's Toughest Rodeos in that role as well as supporting his wife. Mike is the husband of Lori Jo Orman, one of the trick riders Gander had hired to work some of the events.

"My first rodeo of his was in Peoria, Illinois, in 1992 as a field rep," Orman said. "I actually knew Steve before that because Lori had trick rode for him a couple of years prior. I wouldn't say I knew him very well, but we knew each other."

While Lowry was looking for a replacement, Orman knew of other Dodge Rodeo employees that were vying for ownership. When their bid fell out of favor and Gander acquired the program, there were some hard feelings. It got to the point that Orman told others that he didn't think he could ever work for Gander.

"What changed was I think we grew a better respect for one another," Orman said. "When I told him I wasn't interested in working for him, I was a little bit ticked off, but not so much at him."

The two began hashing out their differences during a breakfast meeting in Bellevue, Iowa, a hamlet of 2,300 souls along the Mississippi River in the northeastern portion of the state. Gander wanted Orman to become Dodge Rodeo's general manager.

"Even when we met for breakfast in Bellevue, I would talk about him buying the company, and I was still pretty put out because, at the time, a couple of other employees were trying to buy the business," Orman said. "I guess all my eggs were in their basket, and I was rooting for them. It wasn't necessarily against Steve, but I was disappointed that they weren't actually going to realize their dreams.

"Steve made a promise to me that if I came to work for him as his general manager, he would sell me the company. Even when we first talked about it, he kind of had a five-year vision where that's what he wanted to do."

Gander had a plan, but it was based on what he was doing and what he had hoped for the futures of both Dodge Rodeo and World's Toughest Rodeo.

"I didn't want to run the company day-to-day, and I was only going to be involved on a short-term basis," Gander said. "I had decided twenty years before that I was going to retire after twenty-five years. I was working both ends of the candle. I would ask the office staff, the committees, the PRCA people: 'Which one of the Dodge reps is the best guy to work with?'

"Mike Orman's name kept coming up. I had breakfast one time with him and asked him if he wanted to be the general manager. I said, 'If you do a good job, I'll sell you the company in five years.'

"Mike said, 'Oh, I'll never be able to afford it,' but I told him that I'd make sure he could afford it. We joke now, but I told him one time that I knew he didn't want to work for me, but I didn't let that stop me from asking him."

As he had done with World's Toughest, Gander didn't let many obstacles stand in the way of helping Dodge Rodeo build on its successes. The company's office had been in Marietta, Georgia, just across the way from Dobbins Air Force Base in the Atlanta suburb. The Ormans purchased property in Ottumwa, a community of 25,000 in southeastern Iowa, which became the new home for Dodge Rodeo. Gander moved Dodge Rodeo to Ottumwa and built a new office and warehouse for Orman to manage.

It worked because Gander's hands-off approach allowed Orman to have a more comfortable setting for him to operate the business. Williamsburg, Iowa, was the home of

World's Toughest Rodeo, but it was an hour-plus drive for Orman. His commute shortened, and he was able to handle the operations with great success.

"Steve is one of the most thorough thinkers there is in the sport of rodeo," Orman said of Gander. "He really does try hard to look at all aspects of the sport. You have a conversation about the impacts and benefits, the takeaways, and 'how can we gain here.' You don't just dip your toe in the water. You're always digging a little bit deeper. You could have some pretty deep thinking with him that I didn't have the chance to have with some other people."

Like Gander, Orman took a mindful approach to the work at hand. He was searching for ways to build on a program that had already been defined by excellence, from Lowry to Gander to Orman, who purchased Dodge Rodeo in 2005 and kept the program thriving for another twenty years before the program was discontinued at the end of 2024.

"The thing I liked about Steve was his forward-thinking, looking for something new, trying to lead instead of always following," Orman said. "That's a struggle for the industry, because there are only so many ways you can create change. At World's Toughest Rodeo, I got to see some of his innovations, like having a magician act in a rodeo. He had a wagon that was pulled in with draft horses and made a horse appear in the middle of the arena, which surprised 10,000 people.

"That was very innovative, but we also got to try some of those things and do some of that with Dodge Rodeo. Probably the biggest thing I got from Steve was how to work with employees; how to hear them, listen to them, take their best ideas, and try to use them whenever we could. I think that was something he always wanted to do and was good at. He taught me it would take being a little bit more humble to do that, which wasn't easy for me, but it was the best approach."

Gander provided Orman with the right frame of mind to handle the challenges and fortunes that could come with Dodge Rodeo. With that, he began to ride off into the sunset with retirement as his plan. Alas, it was short-lived. His insights and innovations were needed, especially in rodeo and other Western sports. He listened when others called, and he served as a consultant and more for several years after.

He continued to strengthen the legacy he had built, and others quickly discovered that the benefits of having Steve Gander around were returned twofold.

CHAPTER 12

# GANDER THE CONSULTANT

Steve Gander had done everything he set out to do with World's Toughest Rodeo. With his success came the opportunity to own the Dodge Rodeo program, which he continued to build in the five years he had the company.

It was time. Gander earned his retirement and the chance to sit back and enjoy the trappings of home.

"When I sold World's Toughest Rodeo in 2005, it was the largest privately held rodeo company in the industry based on gross income," Gander said. "My health was the primary reason for selling. My dream was for someone to take it to the next level."

He sold Dodge Rodeo to Mike Orman, who had served Gander as the company's general manager. He sold World's Toughest Rodeo to Tommy Joe Lucia, another Gander understudy. Everything was set up for both entities to have brilliant futures.

It wasn't long, though, before the PBR came calling. The organization, founded in 1992 by twenty bull riders eager to showcase the most popular part of rodeo as a stand-alone sport, had grown in popularity since Gander had ridden into his glory years. Randy Bernard became the PBR's chief executive officer in 1995 and had used his visionary approach to build the brand.

Still, he sought Gander's assistance in expanding the PBR's reach in 2006, just a few months after Gander had closed up shop.

"Randy Bernard asked if I would come to Colorado Springs and work for the PBR," Gander said. "I tried to say no to Randy because I did not feel like I was rested and ready for new ventures, but it's hard to say no to him. This was going to be a short-term project. My job was to open up PBR offices in Canada, Brazil, Mexico, and Australia.

"I truly enjoyed working with Randy and his very competent staff. Working with him was the most wonderful, enjoyable, awesome experience of my life. That guy would say he'd do something, and I would think there was no way in hell it could get done. But Randy got it done. To this day, I am still in awe of what he was able to accomplish."

They both had a purpose, and Gander witnessed Bernard's brilliance up close. During a meeting in Chihuahua, Mexico, the pair met with the city's Chamber of Commerce and the mayor to see about opening an office in town and hiring a bull-riding director. The meeting went well, and the mayor invited the two gringos to his home for dinner.

The following day, Bernard and Gander went to meet with Jose Reyes Baeza Terrazas, the governor from the state of Chihuahua. Prior to that meeting, Gander and Bernard discussed how one objective was to make sure that American bulls could cross the border. After some discussions about the topic, Gander offered some advice.

"I told Randy, 'After the pleasantries are over with and he asks what he can do for you, that might be a good time to bring up how to bring those bulls across the border,'" Gander said. "Sure enough, we sit down on the couches in the governor's office and exchange pleasantries. They were sponsoring a Mexican bull rider, and the conversation was going well. Pretty soon the governor says, 'Well, now, what can I do for you?'

"Randy looked over at me, and I thought he was going to burst out laughing."

With the situation playing out as Gander predicted, Bernard helped accomplish the mission. The governor not only pushed the obstacle to the side, he utilized his strong relationship with authorities at the United States border.

"The PBR bulls had a police escort from the border to Chihuahua," Gander said. "Randy has always amazed me on his courage and ability to get the impossible done."

Gander stayed with the PBR just two months. Outside of Bernard, there was conflict, especially with Sean Gleason, who was the organization's chief operating officer at the time. Gleason has been the PBR's CEO since 2015.

"I got out a little bit earlier than I expected because of Mr. Gleason," Gander said. "I just told Randy that I didn't sell my company to be abused like this. That's too hard. That's too hard on me and too hard on the PBR. I resigned from the PBR."

Bernard and the chief financial officer Dennis Gach tried to get Gander to stay and assured him he wouldn't have to deal with Gleason.

"Dennis said I had gotten more accomplished in two months than they did the previous year."

As had been his modus operandi, Gander made an impact in just sixty days, and the PBR went on to enhance its international presence. A few years later, another longtime player in rodeo reached out, and Gander's marketing powers were exercised on a new stage, the International Finals Rodeo (IFR), the year-end championship for the Oklahoma City-based IPRA.

"The general manager, Dale Yerigan, needed a little assistance marketing the IFR," Gander said. "It was an honor to be approached by Dale, and he and I worked great together. You cannot find a more honest person. His office staff, especially Pam Queen and Carissa Stewart, were always supportive, helpful, and a joy to work with.

"I am proud of their success. One of the changes I made was their logo, the one they use today. Their logo before was too complicated. You couldn't see it, and it wasn't identifiable. It was just an old-time cowboy logo.

"I also designated more of the budget into television and cross promotions, and we restructured their seating scale for ticket sales. I helped with production, and we increased their attendance the first year from 10,000 to 18,000 people, and this was during the 2010 financial crisis where gas prices were high."

The crisis continued for months, and that led into another opportunity for Gander to expand his horizons.

Tom Hicks, owner of the MLB's Texas Rangers and the NHL's Dallas Stars at the time, had owned Mesquite Arena in the Dallas suburb for ten years before selling it to Camelot Sports & Entertainment in 2009. The new owners lost nearly $2 million in eighteen months. They were looking to sell the complex, well known in the region for its rodeos that take place each weekend from July to August.

"I think there were seven other owners at the time, and they were wanting out," Gander said. "I was riding my horse in the desert of Arizona, and Jack Beckman called and said, 'Mesquite Arena needs to be sold and all the deals are falling through; why don't you buy it?' I asked him how much, and he told me.

"I might've had enough money to buy it, but I wouldn't have had enough money to operate it. He asked me if I knew somebody that might be interested. The name I came up with was Stace Smith; I didn't know Stace, but I thought about him because of where he's at. So, I got ahold of him and told him what the deal was and what they were asking."

Smith—who owns both Gulf Shore Tel-Com, a fiber-optics company, and Stace Smith Pro Rodeos, an eleven-time Professional Rodeo Cowboys Association Stock Contractor of the Year—wanted the rodeo to continue. Gander followed Smith's lead to Mesquite in 2011.

"I was asked to evaluate the business," Gander said. "They asked if it could be turned around, or if they'd be better to just walk away from it. After a few days of analysis, I thought it could break even in about two years. Stace asked me when I could start, but I told him I was assisting the IFR and wasn't looking for a job.

"Stace can be pretty persistent. I committed to two years with him. In that time, we increased rodeo business by 45 percent and the non-rodeo event business by 78 percent. We were reaching break-even territory. Within two years, we showed a profit, and that's when gas prices were four dollars a gallon. Families were spending fifty dollars more per month on necessities than what they had before, so it was harder to get that entertainment dollar."

Mesquite Arena was building to what it had hoped to be. Sales were going up, and Gander was hoping to expand as the arena owners took the next step.

"I encouraged them to hire a professional arena manager or an arena-management firm," he said. "I researched several options and recommended they hire Compass Arena, which had a good reputation and success with small- to mid-size arenas. The owners could not make a decision, so I stayed on while they decided what to do.

"I was there three and a half years. They brought in an inexperienced person, chosen because he was cheap and a friend of an owner. I retired. After a cheap guy lost three years of revenue increases, I brought a new buyer to the table, and the arena was sold."

Through his tenure with Mesquite Arena, Gander built relationships that have stood the test of time. One of those is with Deanna Holderith, a former staff member of the PRCA who still lived in Colorado Springs when she got the call about possibly working at Mesquite Arena.

"Steve flew me out so that I could at least come see what it was," Holderith said. "It's funny, because he figured if I came out that I was getting ready to start the job, but I wasn't 100 percent sure I had the job. I pulled up to meet him and the staff and be there for the weekend and see the rodeo and their operation. I liked him as soon as I met him. We got along really well."

Within two weeks, she was beginning the process of moving from the base of Pikes Peak to the Dallas-Fort Worth Metroplex. Their working relationship thrived, as did their social lives. She spent a lot of time with Gander and his wife, Peggy, and their bond forged tightly.

"The thing I love the most about Steve is his good heart, his natural ability to make people feel good," she said. "He wanted to help others do better and help them meet whatever goals that might be or whatever they wanted to accomplish in life. I think it was my first rodeo of the season, and I was talking to him about going home. I grew up in Washington state, and I would go home usually once a year and see my parents and the things that were still there.

"I really didn't think I could leave work, but he called me into the office and handed me a check and told me, 'I'm paying for your trip to Washington to go home. You need to see your family and take a break.'"

Maybe Gander's experiences were making him more mellow. Many of World's Toughest Rodeo staffers talked about his gruffness, especially in the early stages of the company.

Maturity, too, tends to help with one's reactions to the surroundings and the actions of others. But those who know Gander best always point to his genuine nature and his positive influence on their lives.

"He hired a kid straight out of college and gave him an opportunity," Holderith said. "He just wants to give people an opportunity to be successful, and he doesn't want credit for it."

That "kid" is Brady Wilson, who was wrapping up studies at Missouri Valley College and serving as a graduate assistant coach for the rodeo program, which has been led by Ken Mason for several years.

"I asked Ken Mason one day to keep an eye out for me for some young guy that's going to be really good," Gander said. "He told me everything good about Brady. That's kind of the way I find people, just asking around."

It worked. Mason got Wilson in contact with Gander, and it didn't take long before some magic happened.

"I wanted to be in the rodeo business," Wilson said. "I was getting my masters, and Steve had gone to Mesquite the year before. I was needing a job, sort of an internship with the opportunity to learn and make a little bit of money."

That was in February 2012, the same month Wilson got engaged.

"Steve Gander gave me a signing bonus to come down, and I sold a load of hay to move from Missouri down to Texas," Wilson said. "I took that money home, bought a ring, got engaged and moved down.

"Working with Steve was really good. I got to be in some of the meetings with some companies like RAM Rodeo or Wrangler, and some companies outside the industry. I listened to his approach to selling rodeo and what we had to offer. I'd come from the cowboy side of things, the rodeo side of things. I knew a little bit about production from putting on our home rodeo, but my knowledge was pretty limited.

"I knew a little bit about selling sponsorships, but he taught me on a new level as far as what the end-users are looking for. All of a sudden, I looked at it from the audience and the people whose names were on the wall. It changed everything as far as how I think about rodeo and what we have to offer."

That education was priceless, but so were the lessons outside the workplace. Like Holderith, Wilson had a special bond with the Ganders. In fact, Wilson lived on the Ganders' property on the east side of Dallas.

"My horse has stayed at his house," Wilson said. "I probably learned as much on the back porch having a cigar and a scotch as I did working in the office."

That's where he could see the one thing that defines Gander the most: passion. The love affair he has with marketing and promotion and the relationships he has built through rodeo are as strong as ever. He built a brand on it. He took other brands and expanded their purposes.

"People talk about him being a hard-ass or whatever, but I don't think I saw it that way," Wilson said. "I was close to him at the house and spent time with him outside of work, so I understood his passion."

They remain close, in both proximity and their relationship. When Gander had a medical episode while his wife was in Florida photographing Western sports, Wilson was there at the drop of a hat to make sure everything was covered. Wilson made sure Steve was put into medical care, then took care of the place while he was out of service. It was a familial situation for all involved.

"He's very much like a grandfather to my kids," Wilson said. "Seeing him interact with them is way different. They wouldn't even know he could be a boss."

But Gander was the boss. He had the pedigree to prove his merits, but his personality and his relationships were helping him take every step along his path.

"While there are many women who work in rodeo, many still consider it the 'Old Boys Club,'" Holderith said. "Steve did not see it that way. What mattered to him was if you could do the job, and he gave me a chance. He never doubted my ability. He trusted my opinion—whether it was sitting in on interviews with potential new hires, being part of meetings with new partners, or day-to-day operations.

"I knew I was up for the job, but Steve not asking me if I was—just letting me run with it— helped me know that he believed in me and my ability to do it. In the world of the 'Old Boys Club,' that's the biggest compliment he could have ever given me."

That's the thing about a man with not only a genuine soul but also a strong work ethic. He wanted to build on each person's character and find the fire that ignited the best in them. It's one of the many things that made Gander successful, and it's why others kept calling.

"A couple of months after I retired for the third time, the Aksarben Foundation in Omaha, Nebraska, reached out to me," Gander said. "Their famous event had lost over $100,000 each of the past seven years, $150,000 the previous year. They still had a year on their contract with the PRCA to host the Pro Tour Finals; they wanted to honor their PRCA agreement then consider the idea to discontinue hosting the Aksarben rodeo. After I reviewed their financials and ticket sales, they asked, 'Can we break even?'

"I told them, 'If there are no sacred cows, you can have a nice profit.' Then they assured me there were no sacred cows."

Gander knew it was going to take some work, but he was willing to roll up his sleeves and get to it.

"When somebody says there are no sacred cows, there are still sacred cows," he said. "I don't mean that to disrespect the good people I dealt with at Aksarben; they were an absolute honor to work with and were very good people. The sacred cows were among the committee people, the 'volunteers.' It was hard for them to understand that we've got to make money. We can't do something just because we've always done it this way."

Aksarben is a well-established foundation with exceptional community commitment. The sixty volunteers loved rodeo, but the foundation had hired Gander without the committee's involvement. Any suggestion of change was met with great resistance.

"People always want change as long as they are not affected," Gander said. "There were a few rotten apples spoiling what was otherwise a great group of volunteers. I failed to get everyone in the canoe paddling in the same direction. A couple of them were calling the foundation president and the PRCA office with their bullshit. Fortunately, because we were showing plenty of success over previous years, I outwardly maintained the confidence of the foundation officers, or at least I thought so.

"The bottom line is we cut the fat out of the budget and appropriated the money where it was better utilized, greatly increased sponsorship dollars, and grew ticket sales. Aksarben made a $180,000 profit after I was paid my fee, and I'm not cheap. When you consider that they lost $150,000 the year before, that was a $330,000 swing to the positive."

There was still balking from a few of the committee people. They'd gone to the foundation president, who approached Gander during a cocktail reception a few weeks after the rodeo. Gander was praised for the profit. He was then admonished for how his treatment of others was perceived.

"He told me that when he was getting calls about me, he thought maybe I was a sonofabitch (S.O.B.), but now he didn't think I was," Gander said. "I told him I could be an S.O.B. when I needed to be, but I hoped I was a good S.O.B. most of the time.

"It might sound too simple, but I don't have any tolerance at all for the status quo, and I have absolutely no patience for bullshit. There are no good guys or bad guys to me. There are just guys, and we're going to do it. I've never learned to play politics, so things are not gray with me. They're either black or white, and that's good. I'm able to get things done a lot quicker than anybody else, but I ruffle some feathers that way. You can talk to people who worked with me thirty years ago or you can talk to people who worked with me ten years ago, and they were probably all pissed off at me at one point. But now, we're still friends."

For example, take Gander's relationship with Gretchen Kirchmann, who was on the front lines with him in Omaha. She was the director of public relations and sponsorships at Aksarben, and the two began their collaboration when Gander was hired in January 2015. Their offices were next to one another, and they had a bit of history. When Gander was at Mesquite, Kirchmann was the director of public relations for RFD-TV, which was producing The American Rodeo for the first time in 2014. The event's semifinals were at the Mesquite Arena—she only got a glimpse of what Gander was all about then, but they were deep in the mud together in Omaha.

"It was fun; it was difficult," Kirchmann said. "He really challenges the status quo on all sorts of promotions and decisions on marketing. He's also so kind in the fact that he wants to help everyone be better.

"He's originally from Iowa; I'm originally from Minnesota. We know the Midwest, Great Plains, Nebraska kind of demographics of people—neither of us had deep roots in Omaha, but we had deep roots in rodeo promotion and marketing. There was a lot of collaboration because, in the office, we were really the only two that understood the sport of ProRodeo."

She also got a crash course on the Gander approach to promotion and marketing. She was fascinated with how he met with media partners, his thoughts on media-buying, designing, and advertising packets, and working with different associates.

"I feel like I went to Steve Gander State University," said Kirchmann, who owns Kirchmann Media Group. "I was constantly learning from him, and he had practical answers to share.

"The thing I think about Steve is that he's fair to all parties. He's fair to the personnel. He's fair in the sense that he's a professional, and he expects everyone to bring their A game. He can understand how many hours a volunteer has and is able to help make them be the best they can be."

That translated into great successes for the people that trusted Gander with their products, whether it was the PBR, the IFR, Mesquite Arena, or Aksarben.

"I think my employees might have been frustrated with me from time to time, probably every week," Gander said with a slight grin. "But they forgave me for being human because they know that I care."

CHAPTER 13

# THE DOLLOR BET

There weren't many people more famous in the 1950s and '60s than movie star John Wayne.

He was born Marion Robert Morrison in Winterset, Iowa, and his family moved to Glendale, California, when he was about nine years old. He graduated high school there and attended the University of Southern California before getting into a career as an actor.

For youngsters like Steve Gander, Wayne was an icon, especially for boys from Iowa. Steve and his siblings loved Westerns, and luckily, they were abundant during his early years. In the 1950s, Wayne acted in movies like *Searchers* and *Rio Bravo*. A decade later, it was films like *The Comancheros* and *True Grit*. Wayne won the Academy Award for best actor for his portrayal of "Rooster Cogburn."

John Wayne was an imposing figure, someone whose character always seemed to be in the good fight. His talents brought him fame, but his on-screen persona helped him become beloved by millions. Those Iowans? They loved the idea that one of their own had become a household name and someone who epitomized their Midwest culture. He may have spent most of his life in California, but he was very much one of them.

"I was like most of America at the time and still am a big John Wayne fan," Gander said. "Him being an Iowa boy like me helped that a little bit, but there was a lot about him to admire."

Wayne was awarded the nickname "Duke" as a youngster. The family dog was named Duke, and he was a constant companion. Wayne was a regular visitor to the local firehouse, and he always had the dog with him. Firefighters knew the animal's name and started calling the kid "Duke," too. The name stayed with him the rest of his life, even when he was approved for the Congressional Gold Medal on May 23, 1979, just nineteen days before his death.

By then, John Wayne was more of an icon. His final movie, *The Shootist*, was almost real life, reminding fans of the frailty of human existence. Wayne played an aging gunfighter who was dying of cancer. Diagnosed with lung cancer in 1964, he died fifteen years later from stomach cancer.

All the while, he sat tall in the saddle, and the latter part of his career was astride a 1,600-pound chestnut Quarter Horse named Dollor. Six movies like *The Shootist*, *Big Jake*, and *The Cowboys* featured Wayne on the massive, red animal, which was owned by Dick Webb Motion Picture Livestock. Wayne requested Webb keep the horse for him to ride in all future Westerns. It was the only time in his career that Wayne had requested a specific horse.

Dollor was also featured on an episode of *Gunsmoke*, where actor Buddy Ebsen was supposed to ride the horse. Ebsen was getting up in age and Dollor was very tall at 16 hands. The director asked Buck Taylor, who portrayed Newly, to ride Dollor and for Ebsen to ride Taylor's mount.

John Wayne was a movie legend, and Dollor was following suit. The animal had a bit of a following, and the gelding's status wasn't lost on Steve Gander, who realized Dollor could become a benefit to his new start-up, World's Toughest Rodeo.

"There was an ad in Western Horseman magazine saying Dollor was for sale for $35,000," Gander said. "I thought about it. T.L. Bush was really pushing me; he thought it was a great idea."

After pondering, Gander went to his local banker with a creative justification for buying the horse. The plan was to utilize Dollor at World's Toughest Rodeo and create a feature tribute to the actor and legend.

"I told the bank president about John Wayne's horse being up for sale," Gander said. "I figured I could pay for the horse just by what I save not having a specialty act. If I make the horse a specialty act, when I'm done, I can sell the horse. My act is then cheaper for the year, so I'll save money.

"So, I called Dick Webb and told him I was interested in buying the horse. He wanted to know what I was going to do with it, and I told him. He thought it was a good idea, but I said, 'I can only afford $30,000.' He told me there was a guy in France that offered to pay $35,000 and that [entertainer] Wayne Newton was willing to pay $30,000."

Webb didn't think the animal should leave the United States and thought Newton would only put Dollor in a paddock, so he agreed to terms with Gander, who acquired the horse in 1981.

"I paid $30,000, which was a lot of money in 1981 for an unregistered Quarter Horse," he said. "But timing is everything. It was certainly a perfect tie-in to what we wanted to do. It was the right thing to do because we had grown men come over to us and want to touch the horse. John Wayne also had recorded the song 'America, Why I Love Her,' which is what we wanted to use in our tribute."

Acquiring the music wasn't as easy as anyone could imagine at the time. Gander had scoured radio stations looking for the song but failed to have any luck. He went to the Aksarben rodeo in Omaha (years before he went to work for the organization) to visit with members of the Sons of the Pioneers, the band that played with Roy Rogers for many years. Gander's hope was to hire the band for a show he was producing in Ames, Iowa.

"I was talking with Dale Warren of the Sons of the Pioneers in the bar after the rodeo and told him about the horse and my trouble finding the John Wayne song, 'America, Why I Love Her,'" Gander said. "He told me that Billy Liebert produced it, and Billy was the accordion player for the Sons of the Pioneers. Dale goes to the other side of the bar and gets Billy Leibert, so I tell Billy what I'm doing, and he tells me he will send me an album."

While one of the most popular Western actors in movie history, Wayne recited the words with a music backdrop, and that recording was made into vinyl records.

"Back then, it was a 33 [RPMs]-speed album, and about a week later, I got a whole case of these albums by John Wayne," Gander said. "I've still got some of them, and the rest of them I used as special gifts for people."

Dollor was an integral piece of the success Gander had in the early stages of World's Toughest Rodeo. It was a drawing card, for sure, but the tribute hit on a number of emotional ties that rodeo fans had with John Wayne and the well-mannered horse. "America, Why I Love Her" was actually penned by John Mitchum, whom Gander met at a World's Toughest Rodeo in Fort Worth, Texas. John was the brother of the famed actor Robert Mitchum.

"We were doing the rodeo at the Tarrant County Convention Center, and the Sons of the Pioneers were there with me," Gander said. "Before the rodeo, Dale Warren asks if they can have a guest come to the rodeo. It was John Mitchum. Soon after I find out it's him, we do our tribute to John Wayne under the spotlights, and we put the spotlight on John Mitchum and recognize that he wrote the song.

"I guess we did a good tribute to John Wayne with his song because Mitchum had tears in his eyes."

John Mitchum was an American actor with 169 credits in film and television. For the folks in Fort Worth that night, the memory of a songwriter who touched their hearts was just a lasting image of a tribute to remember. The investment Gander had in Dollor was making its mark. He sold the big chestnut in 1983. After his days in the movie industry, Dollor was said to have traveled more than 134,000 miles, and many of them were with the folks at World's Toughest Rodeo.

Gander's time with Mitchum impacted his life. It helped Gander develop relationships, some of which he still holds dearly. He's always had an appreciation for Westerns, and having had the opportunity to meet some stars from his childhood has remained vivid in his recollections.

"I remember growing up, we would get up early and get our chores done on Saturday morning so that we could be in the house by 10 o'clock to watch *Roy Rogers*," Gander said. "After we'd watch the show, we had to go back outside and work, so I grew up greatly influenced by Roy Rogers and the Sons of the Pioneers.

"I've never really been in awe of any entertainer. I've done hundreds of concerts and had many of the biggest names, like Brooks and Dunn and all that, but I rarely had my picture taken with them, never got autographs, and I now regret that totally. I was too busy to do it."

Friendships are forged by relationships—ones built on common ground and caring for one another. They helped develop Steve Gander into the man he is today—a genuine person able to grow personally and professionally. Each exchange became somewhat of a defining position on where he was and where he wanted to be.

"The Sons of the Pioneers were special; they were genuine," Gander said. "So, after the rodeo, they invited me up to their room, and I went with Terry Bush up there. We sat around this room with five or six guys from Sons of the Pioneers, passing around a couple of bottles.

"Well, after two or three sips of Jack Daniels, they weren't stars anymore—we were buddies."

## CHAPTER 14

# SIDE SHOWS

Steve Gander realized early in his creation of World's Toughest Rodeo that ticket-buyers in the Upper Midwest might need something special to draw them to events.

That's why he purchased Dollor, the horse John Wayne rode in some of his movies. Putting on a well-rounded show meant he utilized other entertainment features, like the Sons of the Pioneers, the band that had often accompanied legendary entertainer Roy Rogers.

Gander wasn't afraid to buck the norms in rodeo promotion. Dollor was just one aspect of his early shows, but there were others. In keeping with his Wild West theme in the big cities, he took folks on a trip back in time. Since many Americans had grown up watching Westerns on television and in theaters, Gander knew that aspect was still an attraction to his shows.

Whether it was a tribute to Wayne or celebrating history, he was pushing all the right buttons. Another idea that popped into Gander's brilliant mind came straight off the cutting-room floor. He purchased a stagecoach, which he intended to be used in the openings of his events. It worked.

"The stagecoach was built for the sesquicentennial of Indiana and used just one time," Gander said. "The makers used blueprints from the Smithsonian Institute to build it.

The guy who owned the company that built this stagecoach died shortly after the sesquicentennial, and it sat in a shed, so his wife put it up for sale. I bought it. I also bought a four-horse hitch and used paint horses, and we hauled it around the country."

While he had the stagecoach, Gander utilized it to kick-start his performances, which began with an old-fashioned stagecoach robbery. Actors played their roles to a tee, and it added more flavor to an already action-packed performance. Children stood next to their parents, who sat near the edges of their seats to take in the drama unfolding before them.

It was eye-catching and intense, and it brought into present day what it must have been like to live in the 1800s, when the West was being developed by cowboys, farmers, and other pioneers.

"There was expense to pulling that around the country," Gander said. "It took two rigs: one for the horses, and one for the stagecoach."

Those were the challenges Gander was willing to overcome in order to make his vision become a reality. It was a process he repeated time after time. He once hired an illusionist in a different capacity than many people realized was possible. While many producers would have stationed a magician near the entrance to help greet guests, Gander had grander plans.

"When I decided I wanted to make a horse disappear in the arena, I thought that would be just the most awesome thing to do," he said. "I found this illusionist in Minneapolis and told him what I wanted to do. He said it would be a lot easier to make one appear than disappear. I thought that would be okay, so I hired him. He came down to Iowa, and I'd bought a rubber-tire, fifth-wheel wagon, and I told him I wanted to make it into a prison wagon, and we wanted to make a horse appear.

"I had this vision, and he thought it was great because I wanted to create the bars like a prison wagon that you could see all the way through. He helped me build this wagon and taught me how to do it."

Creating the illusion can be the most painstaking part. The goal is to trick the eyes of the audience members. An elaborate staging system was put into place to hide the horse in the wagon. During the opening, staff member Tommy Joe Lucia would play the role of the sheriff, who would be overthrown by his prisoners. They would put Lucia in the makeshift wagon cell, then cover the vehicle with a tarp to "make the sheriff sweat the deal and bake him in the sun to get rid of him," Gander said.

Smoke would then fill the wagon, and within seconds, Lucia would be astride the mount. A ramp would drop down, and the sheriff chased the bad guys out of the arena.

"It was pretty cool, and we had people see that act two or three times and never figure out how we did it," Gander said. "Bronc Rumford said it was the best thing he'd ever seen in rodeo."

Rumford is a former rodeo cowboy whose father, Floyd, had created Rumford Rodeo Co. Bronc Rumford remains involved in rodeo production at events across the U.S. He pointed out what many saw in the Gander productions; sometimes it takes doing things in a different way to make a big impact on an industry.

Like every "New Coke"—a Coca-Cola reinvention of its longtime consumer favorite that saw it flounder in less than three months in 1985—there are organizations like Netflix, which went from a mail-order DVD-rental business in 1998 to a streaming service today. Some ideas don't work, but others help build tremendous success.

"What Steve did with World's Toughest Rodeo made some other rodeos step up their productions," said Keith Isley, a longtime rodeo clown and entertainer who retired at the end of 2024.

"At the end of it all, it's rodeo entertainment, and you're only as good as the people you work with. I had worked with some really talented people, but World's Toughest Rodeo was top-shelf with its production and timing and all that. It was a production that was unbeatable at the time."

Gander had the vision, something that many other producers wished they had. It's a gift, really. The artist must have imagination to conceive the project before it can be drawn, painted, or sculpted. The creative mind oftentimes works much differently than one that's analytical, but Gander was able to make both sides of his brain coexist.

"He thinks stuff up, and I'd say, 'That's the dumbest thing I've ever heard,'" said David Morehead, co-owner of Three Hills Rodeo and a former World's Toughest Rodeo staff member.

"He would implement it, and none of us wanted to do it, but it turned out to be a bell-ringer. Not everything worked every time, but it usually did.

"Steve's vision in the entertainment business was very rare."

One of the first innovations Gander added to World's Toughest Rodeo production was a show finale. While driving back to Iowa from the IFR in Tulsa, Oklahoma, on a January day in the early 1980s, he was inspired with the idea of producing endings to his rodeos.

"The idea came to me about 2 or 3 a.m.," Gander said. "I was reflecting on just seeing the IFR, which was a great rodeo and had great production. Still, after the last bull bucked and left the arena, the clown, the bullfighters, and the pickup men left, and the show was over. It was anti-climactic. I thought there must be a way to let the audience know the rodeo was over. We need to let the audience know we appreciate that they chose to spend their evening with us, and that's why I decided to produce our rodeo finales.

"Over the years, we created many finales. Some were full of humor. Some were historical. Some were educational. The one copied most by other rodeos was that we turned the bucking-horse herd into the arena. No one matched our production of this. We always had a dark house with fog and spotlights and great music."

With the arena lights off—under a black house—the announcer made a comment to paraphrase the lyrics from the Chris LeDoux song "Mighty Lucky Man." He'd say, "It was a mighty good thing with the Lord looked down on this world and made horses that buck."

The announcer would pause, then the gates opened, and the herd of horses stampeded through fog and spotlights. That was the cue for the announcer to finish the show with another statement of appreciation.

"We respect these magnificent animals as athletes. We hope you do, too. Please drive carful, because we want to see you next year."

House lights came back on, then music, "Turn Out the Lights (The Party's Over)," then "Happy Trails," would play as the audience exited.

"We always wanted to end by telling the audience how much we appreciated them," Gander said. "We were thankful they chose to spend their evening with us."

CHAPTER 15

# OTHER PRODUCTIONS

Throughout his time as a live-event producer, Steve Gander had a simple motto: "Do it right; do it with pride."

It was more of a formula than a motto—more of a starting point than a conclusion. Those seven words stood for everything that mattered to Gander. He built World's Toughest Rodeo through a creative and mindful approach and with great attention to detail. The smallest of things mattered, like picking up trash even if it wasn't someone's job.

Doing it right also meant understanding his own personality. While building World's Toughest, Gander got into it with the PRCA. Because of that altercation, he held a grudge against the PRCA for several years before coming to terms with it.

"At the time I started with the PRCA, I owned one of the few producer cards, something I still have, and with that, a producer could own livestock," Gander said, noting that most animals were owned by stock-contracting companies. "I purchased a few feature bulls, and we called them the Demon Brothers. They were in our TV commercials, and we featured one each night in our production.

"One stock contractor wanted us to hire him for our winter run. When he didn't get the contract, he must've been a bit upset. He told the PRCA office I was using bulls I wasn't supposed to use. When you do something wrong with the PRCA, you get levied with a fine. Anybody can say something bad about you, and you have to pay your fine before you can defend yourself."

He recalled the fine was $7,000. Gander was livid with the situation, the fine, and the way things were handled. Frustratedly, he reached out to Jerome Robinson, who had been a major player in World's Toughest Rodeo for years and had also been on the PRCA board. Robinson made a call and got the situation resolved, but it still took thirty days before Gander's name was cleared and his fine refunded.

"I held a grudge for a long time, but I now know that part of that was my problem," Gander said. "I was impatient. I have no tolerance for the status quo, and I was dealing with the status quo. I don't want to put up with any bullshit, but I was wrong, and they were wrong."

Although the grudge ended—Gander has served in leadership roles and has served on the PRCA board since that altercation—he stuck to his guns. He was invested in his product and understood better than anybody how to build on its successes.

"No one knows your business or your objectives better than you, but you're not as smart as you think you are," Gander said. "When I started and we did these indoor rodeos and had some success, everybody in the world was coming at me and telling me what I needed to do different. The contestants, the PRCA, and different announcers were all telling me what I needed to do, but they didn't know my business as well as I did. They were also only looking at it for two hours of a 24-hour day or two hours out of a week or two hours out of a year.

"I know that I can learn from everybody, but at the same time, I had a pretty good handle on my business. You can't allow somebody else to get you off on a tangent, or you'll get lost. Besides, we were cutting our own trail; if I followed somebody else's trail, how would I know if that person knew where in the hell they were going? If I cut my own trail, I have a better idea of where I'm going."

With that, though, Gander quickly learned how to play by the rule book. It wasn't the status quo; it was a guide. Still, Gander would get frustrated by rules that existed in the PRCA. How he dealt with those frustrations changed over time, thanks in large part to understanding what steps should be taken instead of the steps that had already been taken.

"T.J. Walter used to tell me, 'If you don't like the rule, get it changed,'" Gander said. "I think early on I was impatient; I knew what I thought was right. T.J. taught me a little patience because all of us make the mistake of criticizing the PRCA or any other organization we're involved in because we only look at things from our own perspectives.

"These are very complex things that are the way they are because of what came about in the past. I think you have to learn why things are the way they are and why they're working that way before you can start making changes."

That is one of the many lessons he learned. There were times he had to adjust his thought processes and his behaviors to continue to build on the projects he had.

"If you'd known me in high school, you would have called me 'Wally the Wallflower,'" he said of his shy nature. "I did not stand out at all. I still don't consider myself a leader, but I think when you own a company, it's a role that's thrust upon you. It's like growing up; you evolve. You make a lot of mistakes, and hopefully you learn from some of them. I don't know how else to do it. I don't consider myself charismatic; I consider myself somebody who digs in and gets some work done.

"I always said that you want to hire the right people. They don't have to know anything about marketing, or they don't have to know anything about rodeo. We can teach that. What I can't teach is enthusiasm. I can't teach good work ethic. I can't teach politeness. I can't teach them to be a team member. That's got to be instilled in them before they get here."

As Gander focused on the work at hand, he realized there were other avenues in which he wanted to dabble. He'd found success in producing rodeos; he wanted to try his hand at other entertainment options, so he found his way into the concert business by way of World's Toughest Rodeo.

"Country music got really popular in the late '80s," he said. "I started putting on some country concerts at my events. After I booked the first few, I said, 'I need to find a better way to be more successful at this.'

"I talked to some booking agents and asked a million questions."

In the process, he was learning more about the music industry and what it took to book the right acts at the right times. He was able to work better negotiations for himself during the first quarter of the year. He would ask around to find out which artists were releasing albums in November so their hits would coincide with his rodeo run that began in January.

"I got Brooks & Dunn, Pam Tillis, and Neal McCoy," Gander said. "Brooks & Dunn had their first hit, and we had 12,000 people come to that rodeo and concert. Neal McCoy was with us when his song 'No Doubt About It' first went to number one in 1994. We created a little niche and found a way to capitalize on it.

"You've got to study and learn. First you have to have the thought to consider it, then you've got to ask a lot of questions. Pretty soon, these guys had this hit song and were wanting twice the amount of money that we were paying. That's when I quit doing it; it was no longer cost-effective.

Everybody learned what we were doing, and the agents were catching on, so I quit doing it."

He also produced nearly sixty concerts that weren't associated with rodeo, but that was just another entity that made Gander the epitome of a promoting genius. That was his business, and his livelihood had been good. Most of his work took him out of Williamsburg, Iowa, but his imagination helped him give back to the people in the community he called home for so long.

"It was the mid-1980s, and the farm economy was really bad," he said. "A guy from the local Chamber of Commerce came to my office and wanted me to buy a membership to the Chamber. I was pretty naïve because I'd never been associated with one, so I asked, 'What does the Chamber of Commerce do?' He told me that it was to promote the town, and I asked how, but he didn't have an answer for me. I said, 'If you come up with an answer that shows me how my money is being spent, I'll buy a membership.'"

It may have been a brilliant way to send the solicitor onward, but it didn't stop Gander's mind from racing. As he sat in his second-floor office overlooking the town square with its brick streets, he pondered more about the chamber's query.

"One of my pet peeves is someone who complains but doesn't do anything about it," he said. "I was visualizing the hard times and the idea that the town needs to be invigorated. We need to get people moving here. How do we get them here?

"I started thinking about the idea that people my age like '60s rock, and I envisioned this beach party on the square. I wrote up a few things and presented it to the city council and suggested we do a beach party. It didn't end up being on the square."

The idea was established. The next step was to make it come to fruition, but like he'd done with every aspect of his business before, Gander faced some opposition. The community's older generation was against it because the folks didn't want a Woodstock in Williamsburg—Woodstock was a music festival on a farm in upstate New York in 1969 that featured some of the top rock artists of the day and had an audience of nearly a half million people. It became an example of the counterculture of the 1960s and those that opposed the Vietnam War.

That kind of show wouldn't go over well in conservative, rural mid-America. Gander knew that; he'd been producing wholesome rodeos for several years, so he understood the culture of people that he hoped to attract. With that, he took his proposal to the people, meeting at the senior center and other community outlets so that he could bring his voice to as many folks as possible.

"I told the seniors, 'If we don't do something to revitalize this town and get people moving into it, these beautiful brick streets will have grass growing through them,'" he said. "I won the senior center over, then the Des Moines Register came and were critical, but we knew what day they were coming. I had them meet us out where the beach party site was going to be, and I had a couple senior citizens and some little kids there, and I talked about it being a family event.

"We won everybody over, and the governor ended up coming."

It was unique enough that the beach party attracted national news.

"*Time* magazine called me up and wanted to know why I thought a beach party was a good idea and why it would work," Gander said. "*Time* wrote a one-page article on it, and I told them that my generation grew up with '60s music, and we have moved into decision-making positions and were exerting our influence. I told them that we were going to see the colors of the '60s for the next couple of years."

He was right.

"Over seven years from 1986-92, we raised over $100,000 for charities and service organizations in a town of 2,000 people."

CHAPTER 16

# WORLD'S TOUGHEST BEYOND GANDER

When it was time for Steve Gander to retire in 2005, his first step was to sell his businesses.

That meant World's Toughest Rodeo was going to be owned by someone else. It was a tad bittersweet for the Iowa man; he'd put everything he had into making his rodeo company a success. He even formed the foundation through his brilliance, stacking his dreams on pillars he'd erected himself.

Gander built trust in his brand. The coworkers were first, but it quickly spread to building managers, sponsors, and ticket-buyers. They knew the product and understood what it was bringing not only to the sport, but also to its contestants and the cities that showcased the events. When it was time to pass along his baby, Gander reached into his history to help World's Toughest Rodeo build toward its future.

Tommy Joe Lucia had spent his formative years with World's Toughest, first as an entertainer, then handling the operations, logistics, and production. He ventured on to the PBR, where he was vice president of events and production, and he was in charge of all aspects of the touring show and the subsequent television program that showcased the PBR's premier tour. He was instrumental in the organization's growth in the seven years he was with the PBR.

He seemed to be the perfect fit to take World's Toughest Rodeo to the next level, so Lucia acquired it from Gander. He then got into a partnership with Jac Sperling of Grit Rock Ventures LLC, where Lucia also served as president of Grit Rock Rodeo LLC. Besides World's Toughest Rodeo, Grit Rock produced the Wrangler ProRodeo Tour and Ariat Playoffs—and their broadcasts—for three years while also producing the reality series *Toughest Cowboy*. The program aired on Spike TV (which became the Paramount Network in 2018) and featured twelve cowboys competing each week in bareback riding, saddle bronc riding, and bull riding.

Grit Rock ran World's Toughest Rodeo through 2011, then it was sold to David Morehead, an Iowa-based livestock producer whose family operates Three Hills Rodeo and Three Hills Ranch Inc. The Moreheads provided stock for World's Toughest Rodeo for several years leading up to that point.

"I was fortunate enough to be able to buy the company," David Morehead said. "Even after we bought it, we would consult with Steve. Sometimes we paid him, sometimes we didn't. But to this day on many things, we still consult with Steve. Up until the last venue that we marketed and produced World's Toughest Rodeo, we would talk to him semi-weekly if not daily."

Morehead began partnering with Miller International, a Colorado-based clothing retailer popularized by its Cinch Jeans and Shirts brand—in 2017, then sold World's Toughest Rodeo to Cinch in 2023.

In the late 1980s, Rorey Lemmel was introduced to World's Toughest Rodeo. He was a bull rider trying to make a living in a game he loved.

"I competed at them back in the day," said Lemmel, now the owner of Harper and Morgan Rodeo and the general manger and producer for the Cinch World's Toughest Rodeo. "They used to have Dodge bounty bulls at them. I remember I rode one, a Burns (Rodeo) bull at the Met Center, and the Dodge rep was a guy by the name of Mike Orman, who went on to own Dodge Rodeo.

"They were good then, and they continue to be good now. I guess we just followed along the trail that Steve made. When Dave Morehead had it, Cinch got involved with the sponsorship. With me previously riding at the rodeos, I knew they were great events, and I was always interested in purchasing them. I ended up being a partner for a little bit before buying them out. It was really good."

Originally from the tiny village of Mud Butte, South Dakota, Lemmel started competing in the PRCA on his permit in 1988. He became a full-fledged member of the association in 1989 and competed mostly in the 1990s. It was then that he got the idea to be involved in the sport in a more organizational sense.

"I dabbled with production at the end of my riding career," he said. "Since I was doing it while I was still riding, I just kept growing in the different roles.

"At the time, I started doing some events, and then it grew into some bigger events. I worked for Stace Smith, and that was really good. I got around some good people with Scotty Lovelace, Pete Carr, and Stace, and I learned everywhere I went by just watching how they did things and pretty much developed my own style."

That approach is more contestant-focused; the idea is to produce an event that benefits the cowboys, and the rest of the entertainment package will follow suit. The 2025 ProRodeo season included nine Cinch World's Toughest Rodeo events—from Des Moines, Iowa, to Charlottesville,

Virginia. Just as it did when Gander started the tour in 1980, the modern version still features the sport's top cowboys.

The format is a bit different than a traditional rodeo. World's Toughest features only the three roughstock events: bareback riding, saddle bronc riding, and bull riding. For a time, it also included barrel racing, but the focus on three events has been a mainstay for the tour for a long time. There are a lot of reasons for it, but part of that decision-making involved the logistics of producing events in arenas that were typically in the downtown areas of cities.

Timed-event contestants like barrel racers travel the circuit in elaborate rigs with living-quarters trailers that allow them to reside on the road comfortably while also being able to care for their horses. Guiding those massive vehicles on city streets then parking in proximity to the stadium can be a nightmare. By eliminating barrel racing from the format, organizers and arena managers are able to focus on the event instead of the logistics surrounding travel.

"When I first started going to them, they were sanctioned, full rodeos," Lemmel said. "They would overrun the buildings, which couldn't handle all the trailers where they were going."

Roughstock cowboys tend to travel with their equipment, even if that means flying on a commercial airline with a saddle and a gear bag. If they drive to an event from southwestern Oklahoma to Winston-Salem, North Carolina, they'll likely fill a vehicle with their bronc-busting buddies and split the costs.

"It's an interesting format when you've got possibly the three most exciting events in rodeo," Lemmel said. "I think that's what draws people. They're in a market such as they don't get the Western lifestyle quite as often as those of us from the Midwest and the West, so I think that's attractive.

"If you walk out my back door in South Dakota, there's a rodeo at nearly every town, so it's a lot different when you go into these cities."

That notion is what set the wheels in motion for Steve Gander. It's why he opted for events in the first quarter of every year in cities that normally didn't see a reflection of the Old West on a regular basis. Those from an urban setting were still enthralled by what they saw on television, whether it was *Gunsmoke* or *Bonanza* or *Yellowstone*.

"I think Steve was 100 percent right," Lemmel said. "I noticed I have better luck going into events that are in bigger buildings. They damn well cost more, but you can sure get a lot of reward out of it. That's what Steve did so well when I went to them events. He went to Buffalo, New York, Indianapolis, Cleveland, and Atlanta. Those places just ain't overrun with rodeo."

That's why Lemmel and Cinch have pushed the product in a more eastern direction. Half of the 2025 schedule included events on the East Coast. Sure, there are old haunts like St. Paul, Minnesota, and Columbus, Ohio—but Raleigh, North Carolina, has drawn some amazing crowds.

"We just need to try to keep pace with our own rate to make rodeo successful for both the committees and the cowboys," he said. "Just grow the sport, and the media has done a great job with that. Sure, there are some growing pains with it, but that's what World's Toughest does so good. It takes us back East, where you never know where the next cowboy is coming from or where the next band is coming from.

"I feel like we have it covered in the West, but the East is where we need to go, and that's why World's Toughest has always been ahead of its time."

That's a benefit Gander instilled in the brand from the beginning. Be groundbreaking. Be innovative. Push the boundaries.

"You've got to give credit to Steve," Lemmel said. "Steve wasn't everybody's flavor of the month and probably wasn't mine when I was a contestant. He damn sure ran a tight ship and was a visionary in starting these events. He was maybe a little hard on the contestants; he'd holler at you and tell you to duck down behind the chutes, something you don't think about as a contestant. Hell, he was just trying to make a living and sell as many tickets as possible, and he was able to do that because he was always looking out for the fans.

"Probably the most amazing thing is that it's still relevant all these years later. It's still man vs. beast. The Wild West comes to the big city. There's an old saying: 'I think there's a little cowboy in all of us.' I think Steve played on that all those years, and it's still that way. I think it's even more prevalent today. It seems like America goes one way and then another way, but it always goes back to the basics that, hell, it still needs a cowboy to help make the world go 'round."

Just like everything else, rodeo has changed dramatically over the years. Technology has come into contention. When Lemmel was playing the game, cowboys learned about the animals with which they were matched via word of mouth or by seeing the animal in action. There wasn't much game planning then. Using one's memory and the memories of others was the most reliable setting. In the mid-2020s, there were smartphone apps that were put into use and a chance to watch a video of a bucking animal moments before it's time to ride.

The Born to Buck program has also exploded. Generations of bucking sires breed to bucking mares, and the results are bettering animal athletes overall. It's not that there weren't great bucking animals in the 1980s; there were. There are just more of them in today's rodeo lineup. Certain stallions are matched with certain mares, and veterinarians will oftentimes use artificial insemination and even perform an embryo transfer from an athletic female into a broodmare, which simply carries the foal to term; the foal is genetically tied to the mare that had been bred.

To take this a step further, Dr. Gregg Veneklasen, an established veterinarian and genetics specialist at Timber Creek Veterinary in Canyon, Texas, has successfully cloned several outstanding bucking geldings, male horses that no longer have the genitalia to breed. Science and technology will continue to impact the sport in many ways.

As technology changes the sport's landscape, World's Toughest Rodeo is always building toward the future. Lemmel would like to see his tour nearly double in the coming years and include a championship event to which only the upper echelon of contestants qualify. While the ultimate goal for all contestants competing in ProRodeo is to qualify for the National Finals Rodeo each year and battle for the elusive world championships in each event—adding a World's Toughest Rodeo finale would go a long way toward that.

The precedent has been established; in 2005, the PRCA created the Xtreme Bulls Tour, which features a finale. The Xtreme Broncs Tour was developed in 2016, and that tour's championship has taken place in Rapid City, South Dakota, every year since 2019.

"Hell, I think there should be a steer wrestling championship and a calf-roping championship," Lemmel said. "The bronc riding finals have turned out to be very successful, and Xtreme Bulls has been very successful. Until everybody's able to retire from rodeo—literally retire and not have to find other jobs to make ends meet—then I think the more money we can put up for these guys is better for all of us. It will start putting us more on par with the other major sporting events.

"That's where I want to go. The more things these guys can do to help them set up for the rest of their lives is where we need to go. These guys are in the prime of their lives to do this, and they have to put the money together when they can."

Rodeo will likely always be a sport outside of the mainstream, but the financial reward for its combatants is getting better. The 2024 world standings featured seven cowboys with earnings of $400,000 or more. Compare that to the major league sports like baseball, basketball, hockey, and football, and the salaries pale in comparison. There are a number of reasons for that, but it primarily comes down to the overall fan interest and the limited opportunities to see teams play throughout a given year.

The average home attendance for the Denver Broncos is nearly 76,400 people, and there are eight to nine home games in Empower Field at Mile High. That's 650,000 people in the stadium for NFL games each year, not including the playoffs. Add to that the network television packages that pay the NFL and its teams, and it's a multi-billion-dollar industry. Compare that to rodeo's thousands of events across North America in a given year but not often at large coliseums. There are a handful of rodeo performances each season in a major complex that seats tens of thousands of fans, like the Houston Livestock Show and Rodeo. It takes place annually at NRG Stadium; RodeoHouston and the Houston Texans are co-tenants of the massive complex that can seat more than 70,000 fans during the rodeo.

While there aren't any multi-million-dollar contracts awaiting competitive cowboys and cowgirls, the financial incentives are growing. Still, there's another big difference between rodeo and mainstream sports. While members of the Dallas Cowboys are not only guaranteed salaries, their business expenses also are covered by the team. Rodeo cowboys must pay for their own costs, and to add to the fray, they also dole out a fee to compete at each event. Neither of those facts will change in the Wild West sport, so the dollars that come as a reward for success are even more valuable.

Two Utah titlists, saddle bronc rider Ryder Wright and bull-rider Josh Frost, earned nearly a half a million dollars each in 2024. Wright closed out his season with $479,957; that's almost $200,000 more than he earned in 2017, when he won the first of three world championships. Frost, who won his first gold buckle after finishing as the runner-up three years in a row, earned more than $400,000 for the third straight year.

"I would say the reason those guys won that much money is because of the people that came before me and my generation," Lemmel said. "Those guys deserve every nickel they get, and it has been so great. When I talked to people I rodeoed with or the Tom Millers and John Forbes who were before my time, they'd do it all over again.

"They didn't make much money while they were doing it, and they were the stars of our game. I think everybody that's ever rodeoed feels that these guys deserve everything they get, and I hope they start making a lot more."

The opportunities to do that are greater than ever because events like World's Toughest Rodeo continue to up the ante. Rorey Lemmel is just carrying on a legacy that Steve Gander began decades before, and Lemmel is following Gander's vision for forward-thinking and innovation.

Those are things that help build a product that takes a sneak peek into the past while also building toward its future. Gander created a modern version of an old Western, and the vision he had in 1980 has continued to thrive decades later.

"I always said that one of my scorecards in building a successful company is that the company must be able to survive after me," Gander said. "We can check that box off."

CHAPTER 17

# THE GANDER TWILIGHT

By the early 1990s, Peggy (McPeak) Miller had made her presence known as a cowgirl.

She was a barrel racer—and an occasional team roping heeler—who earned one of just a handful of spots at the Great Lakes Circuit Finals Rodeo, a regional championship that featured only a dozen ProRodeo cowgirls who were primarily from the states of Missouri, Iowa, Minnesota, Wisconsin, Illinois, Kentucky, Indiana, Ohio, and Michigan.

She also earned qualifications to the WPRA World Finals, the season-ending event for the contestants in the Women's Professional Rodeo Association (WPRA). To earn trips to any annual finale, competitors must beat most of the ladies in the field, and she was doing that regularly.

She traveled the rodeo trail with her good friend, Rhoda Bennon, and both were frequent flyers at World's Toughest Rodeos. That's where Peggy Miller met Steve Gander, the producer of those events in the bigger cities in the upper Midwest. At Bennon's urging, Peggy and Steve went on their first date while at a World's Toughest Rodeo in Richfield, Ohio, a community of about 3,700 folks tucked between Cleveland and Akron.

"I was a little against the date at first," she said. "He was the event producer, and I really didn't know him, but Rhoda convinced me, and that was that."

Steve and Peggy have been together ever since that day in early 1992. After dating eight years, they married during the 2000 NFR in Las Vegas.

"Peggy was that rare combination of beauty and intelligence," Steve said. "She helped me mature . . . a little. We have a lot of fun. We've had only one argument, but it has lasted more than twenty-five years. I have hopes of eventually winning that argument."

He laughed at that statement, but the truth behind it is the two mesh well. At the time, though, it was a big step for both divorcees.

"When I was building my company, I was so engrossed in it and didn't do anything other than work for my company. The only people I met were people that would come to my rodeos, and I didn't really want to date a barrel racer. Peggy was the only barrel racer I've ever asked out."

The date—which was to a Winking Lizard restaurant in northern Ohio—seemed to have worked, but why did it take so long to finally get hitched?

"We started dating and got close, and it was probably a year later that we got engaged but just never found the time to get married," Peggy said. "Everyday life was happening, and we just never found the time because we were both so busy. We were in Vegas for the NFR and finally just said, 'We're going to make time here in Vegas.'"

They flew in their children, which included Peggy's sons, Greg and Travis, and Steve's daughter, Sarah. It was the perfect moment to celebrate their lives together and start a future. It was just a symbol of a life they were already sharing, both as a couple and as coworkers. Peggy was still competing when she took on roles with World's Toughest Rodeo, so she had to manage both aspects of her life and personality.

"I first started helping out with production," she said. "I was helping with the horses, working with the flag girls, doing the openings, and helping however else I was needed. Of course, Steve wrote all the openings, and we just talked about those together. I was also in charge of our merchandising. As we got more rodeos, we had some double-ups, and I'd pretty much oversee everything at one of those sites."

Double-ups were two events in a weekend, and World's Toughest Rodeo was spread across the country at times. Steve needed someone he trusted to run one of the stops, and nobody was more well-suited for it than Peggy.

"He would go one way, and I would go the other," Peggy said. "I was in charge of the rodeos I was at.

"Even when we were working at the same venue, we traveled separately most of the time. I drove the merchandise trailer. He would go into the town a little bit earlier to do some advance promotion, and I would come later with the merchandise trailer and my horse, because I continued to barrel race the whole time I was working there."

The trailer was a gooseneck shell that was filled with all the merchandise—shirts, hats, koozies, and anything else Gander and his team thought they could sell. Peggy's horse was stationed behind the boxes.

"We'd travel all day or all night to get to where we had to go, then we would start doing the preparation," she said. "I guess I was also in charge of setting up the arena, putting up the banners, and just helping the crew. The nice part of that was that we had an awesome crew.

"I always felt like I was a crew member. Everybody worked together. I never felt like a boss, because I wasn't. I was a coworker with everyone."

The couple made it work, but it wasn't without concern. Neither wanted their family life to interfere with the working relationships they had with the rest of the team.

"My initial concern was nepotism, because I didn't want Peggy to expect favoritism and let that interfere with the crew," Steve said. "It was something we talked about all the time, but Peggy worked well with the crew. They loved her, and she took a lot of stress off me."

"It took me a while, but I always made sure to get my work done," Peggy said. "I would hang the banners, and, of course, I had to ride my horse because I was in competitive mode, too. One night when I was riding my horse, Steve walked out and told me what else I needed to be doing. I told him that I would but that right then, I was getting my horse rode.

"That didn't go well, so I got off my horse and hung my banners, but I was mad at him. When I got back to the hotel, he was friendly and asked me about my day, but I didn't want to talk to him.

"Sometimes I felt like he carried the boss mode too far, but that was our relationship and we both learned. I never wanted there to be favoritism in any of the crew's eyes, and the crew knew that. They knew they could tell me things confidentially, and it wouldn't go to Steve, because I was in crew mode, not husband-wife mode."

The important factor was communication between the two. They made sure to hash out their differences and work to the betterment of not only their relationship but their cohesiveness as a team working to produce the best World's Toughest Rodeos they could.

"We knew he had his role, and I had mine," she said. "I acted as an employee in those situations. I didn't try to pull the, 'I'm your wife' thing or the 'I'm your girlfriend' thing, because it didn't fly with him. It didn't fly with me either, so that was a good thing. I wanted to be part of that crew because I really loved that crew."

After working as part of a critical team for so long, there were ties that bound them all together. They laughed and cried, igniting a bond that was crucial to each of their souls. By the time 2005 came around and Steve put both Dodge Rodeo and World's Toughest Rodeo up for sale, his bride was experiencing a bit of mourning.

"It was tragic for me because I felt like I lost part of my world," Peggy said. "I was very close to the crew, and I thought I might never see them anymore. It was very hard. Steve wanted to retire at fifty-five, so that's where he came from. I thought, 'You will never retire at fifty-five, but you just go right ahead.'

"He stayed involved with both companies after he sold them, and I actually stayed involved for another year. That helped me let go because it wasn't just cut off. I felt like I'd lost all those relationships and friendships. I felt like everything was gone, but in reality, it wasn't. We stayed friends with the crew, and I still rodeoed and found other jobs."

Steve's retirement didn't last long. Within months, he'd been summoned by the PBR, and other companies soon followed, seeking his talents and years of experience.

"I thought it was great for him because he was a man with a mind that was not going to rest, and he needed something else," Peggy said. "I think he enjoyed the other ventures. It left me more at home alone and taking care of stuff at the ranch."

That changed a few years later when her husband took a job with the Mesquite Arena in the Dallas-Fort Worth metroplex. Steve was gone more often and for longer than a few days. He'd return to their place in Williamsburg once a month, and Peggy would head south when she could.

Over time, they realized how much they enjoyed the Texas lifestyle. The weather was certainly warmer than northeastern Iowa, and there were other opportunities for them.

"We both decided we liked the job down there, and I enjoyed the area," she said. "I was excited about moving to Texas. Steve was more attached to the Iowa home than I was because I'd only lived there from 1993 until we sold it. I did love it there, but I just thought it would be a great new adventure for us to move to Texas."

They settled on a spot in Rockwall, a community northeast of Dallas. They've made it their home and found ways to continue to develop their relationship. Steve isn't always in business mode as he once was. He's more relaxed, but a big part of that is he no longer has the weight and financial burden that came with operating his own companies.

"As we age, I guess, we either grow apart or together," Peggy said. "When he sold the companies, we had a little more time after we moved to Texas, and we grew together as a couple. That was a really great feeling."

By the mid-2020s, she was more in tune with her own business. As owner of Cowboy Images, Peggy is a photographer who divides her time between various horse shows and rodeos. That keeps her busy, whether she's shooting a hunter jumper event in Florida or a rodeo in New Mexico.

With her on the road, that means the two are apart some throughout a year. When the opportunities allow, Steve jumps in the rig and accompanies his bride at the shows.

"I feel like my life is very fast-paced," she said. "I am home the month of May, and that's about the only time I do not travel. I've finally gotten to where I've taken time off the months of November or December, but with all my travels, I'm gone a lot.

"It's kind of a role-reversal. When we had the rodeo company, he traveled all summer long, and I was home. Now, he's home all summer, and I'm traveling for work. I think we both realized what it was like for the other one in the past. He now realizes what it's like to stay home. That's one of the things that's changed for us, and I think we have a better understanding of each other because of it."

They've found a way to make their lives together—and separate—work for them. It's a mix similar to every other married couple. They are two people with different personalities and likes. Much like how their relationship blossomed while working together, they've found ways to make things work.

"It's like the good and the bad," Peggy said. "I miss him a lot when I'm on the road, but then when I'm home for a while, he'll be like, 'Well, why don't you go back on the road?'"

She laughed, remembering the times she thought the same thing. That's married life in a nutshell and a reason why they've made it work for so long.

Their love affair began after she followed Steve around on the traveling road show that was World's Toughest Rodeo. It continues because he now tags along with her. There are several times throughout the year that he's with her as she handles her business, enjoying the freedom a retired man has earned.

"He comes with me to a lot of the rodeos I go to now," she said. "We take the truck and trailer, and he does all the driving. When we get there, he helps me set up lights. In the middle, he socializes with everybody while I'm working. At the end, he'll tear down the lights.

"He laughs about it now because he says, 'I started my rodeo career setting up and tearing down, and now, by God, I'm ending my career setting up and tearing down, but it's for her.'"

That is Steve's sign of love. He's always been willing to work for something, especially when those things bring out his fire and his passion. He displayed that as a young boy knee-deep in mud and shit while helping on the family farm in northeastern Iowa. He showed it again when he arrived at Donnie Burkholder's place to do the work necessary for a chance to ride bucking horses.

He made a living as a door-to-door salesman, then set records in the seed business before chasing his rodeo dreams and building an empire that still stands on a platform he constructed. He produced events for statesmen, dignitaries, and the President of the United States, while helping countless others build upon a shared passion for a sport created out of the Wild West.

Steve Gander invested his heart, his soul, and his money into creating a brand of entertainment that has sparked the imaginations and the spirits of millions of spectators, all while leaving behind a legacy that will outlive him.

## ABOUT THE AUTHORS

# TED HARBIN

Ted Harbin is one of only eight who have been recognized for his media excellence by both the Professional Rodeo Cowboys Association (PRCA) and the Women's Professional Rodeo Association (WPRA), the top two sanctioning bodies in rodeo. He won the PRCA's Media Award for Excellence in Print Journalism in 2010 and the WPRA's Media Award in 2014. Harbin began his journalism career while attending Pratt (Kansas) Community College and Fort Hays (Kansas) State University, then worked twenty-two years in the newspaper business.

He worked at small weeklies and large dailies before 2005, when he developed TwisTed Rodeo, a media relations company that works primarily in rodeo. In addition to his work being published in hundreds of newspapers, Harbin has written pieces for *Western Horseman, Texas Monthly, the WPRA Magazine,* and the National Cutting Horse Association's publication, *Chatter Magazine.* He has served as media director for many rodeos, stock contractors, and other rodeo entities, and has been a publicist for dozens of cowboys and cowgirls. Harbin is one of the most recognized journalists in rodeo today.

# STEVE GANDER

Steve Gander is the Oz of rodeo, the man behind the curtain who orchestrated his brand of rodeo in ways that nobody had ever seen before. He developed World's Toughest Rodeo, then marketed and promoted his product outside the norms of Western sports. He had video replay before anyone else had considered it. He took rodeo into the big cities like Minneapolis, Chicago, and Cleveland, and introduced the Old West to city folks in a way that entranced them and brought them back for more. His innovations are still being used by producers of thousands of events across North America. The man who produced the Command Performance Rodeo for President Reagan in 1983 will be an influence on the sport for years to come.

He remained active in rodeo years after he "retired," having consulted with multiple organizations to help them better produce and market a profitable experience. He remained on the board of directors for the PRCA and has served as a key facilitator as the sport has flourished over recent years. He has seen World's Toughest Rodeo—the brand he created decades ago—continue to succeed more than twenty years after he sold it.

www.ingramcontent.com/pod-product-compliance
Lightning Source LLC
Chambersburg PA
CBHW031955080426
42735CB00007B/403